# OPEN THE GATES
## to the
# IVY LEAGUE

# OPEN THE GATES
## to the
# IVY LEAGUE

## A PLAN B FOR GETTING INTO THE TOP COLLEGES

C. W. Henderson

PRENTICE HALL PRESS

**PRENTICE HALL PRESS**
**Published by the Penguin Group**
**Penguin Group (USA) Inc.**
**375 Hudson Street, New York, New York 10014, USA**

USA I Canada I UK I Ireland I Australia I New Zealand I India I South Africa I China

Penguin Books Ltd., Registered Offices: 80 Strand, London WC2R 0RL, England
For more information about the Penguin Group, visit penguin.com.

OPEN THE GATES TO THE IVY LEAGUE

ISBN: 978-0-399-16430-9

An application to catalog this book has been submitted to the Library of Congress.

First edition: August 2013

PRINTED IN THE UNITED STATES OF AMERICA

10  9  8  7  6  5  4  3  2  1

*Text design by Tiffany Estreicher*

While the author has made every effort to provide accurate telephone numbers, Internet addresses,
and other contact information at the time of publication, neither the publisher nor the author
assumes any responsibility for errors, or for changes that occur after publication. Further,
the publisher does not have any control over and does not assume any responsibility
for author or third-party websites or their content.

Most Prentice Hall Press books are available at special quantity discounts for bulk purchases for sales
promotions, premiums, fund-raising, or educational use. Special books, or book excerpts, can
also be created to fit specific needs. For details, write: Special.Markets@us.penguingroup.com.

# Contents

## SIGN UP FOR UPDATES ON
## COLLEGE ADMISSIONS

You can sign up for updates on college admissions
and back gateways into top colleges at:

www.openthegates.com

# Introduction

## What This Is and Why I Wrote It

*I am the master of my fate:*
*I am the captain of my soul.*
—WILLIAM ERNEST HENLEY,
"INVICTUS," 1888

L et me throw some numbers at you. Sorry, they aren't very pretty.
We've all heard about the 1 percent versus the 99 percent. It is true that, as of 2009 (the most recent year with firm figures), 35.6 percent of U.S. wealth was in the hands of just 1 percent of the American people. Bad news for most of us, but it actually gets worse. The next richest 4 percent of the American people claim a 27.9 percent chunk of the wealth. Go down a tier to the 15 percent of Americans just below the top 5 percent, and an additional 23.7 percent of U.S. wealth is accounted for. This leaves only a 12.8 percent sliver of the U.S. money pie for nearly eight in ten Americans.

Go to work fresh out of high school, and you can expect to earn a lifetime total of some $1.2 million. Walk through a college gate, and you enter a life in which you will come close to doubling that at $2.1 million. If the gate opens onto a school of the Ivy League, the lifetime number leaps to nearly $3 million.

And you don't even have to wait all your life for the big numbers to kick in. The median starting salaries for Ivy League graduates are 32 percent higher than those of "traditional" liberal arts college graduates. Fast-forward ten or more years, and the difference increases to 34 percent. A recent survey by the global compensation data provider PayScale Inc. of 1.2 million bachelor's degree graduates with a minimum of ten years' work experience revealed very little correlation between the graduate's major and his or her long-term earning power. However, *where* the degree was earned made a very big difference. PayScale revealed that English majors who graduated from Harvard University earned a median starting salary of $44,500, compared to $35,000 for those with English degrees from Ohio State University. After ten years, Harvard English majors were raking in $103,000 annually in median pay, 111 percent more than their Ohio State counterparts.

## WHERE LEADERSHIP BEGINS

Any way you look at the numbers, the conclusion is inescapable. *Going* to college and *where* you go to college are the two most important determinants of your lifetime capacity to create wealth. So, do you choose to brand yourself *victim* or *leader*? If your choice is option two, choose your college very ambitiously, because it is where leadership begins.

The schools this book is dedicated to helping you enter are among the schools whose graduates regularly triple their income and, very often, earn beyond that.

Because—again, based on the numbers—you *do* need help. Writing for *Registered Rep.* ("College Planning Mythbusters," March 1, 2011), college consultant Lynn O'Shaughnessy cites a recent UCLA study showing that "79 percent of the current crop of college freshmen got into their No. 1 choice." Why, then, do so many of us have the impression that it's getting harder than ever to get into college? "The reason why this myth persists," O'Shaughnessy explains, "is because a tiny percentage of institutions in this country—mostly in the Northeast—are nearly impossible to crack." According to *U.S. News & World Report*, Ivy League schools on average reject some 90 percent of applicants. Do the math. Ninety percent puts you distressingly close to a 100 percent certainty of joining the vast majority the Harvards and the Yales turn away.

## UNCONQUERABLE

There is no denying that an Ivy League or other elite diploma has been the seed of many a 1 percent dream. It's true, too, that Americans in the bottom 99 percent have not given up dreaming. It's just that, these days, they are also doing the math. You won't find this must-solve problem on the SAT, but it goes something like this:

- Let the Ivy League and other elite schools educate less than 1 percent of the population.
- Let 35.6 percent of all wealth go to just 1 percent of the population.
- Let a top-flight college education be the single greatest determinant of lifetime income.
- Calculate your chances (or your child's chances, or your grandchildren's chances) of ascending into the 1 percent (or even the top 20 percent) holders of American wealth.

Daunting as the terms of this problem are, they get even harder every year because the population of college-bound students continues to grow, yet the number of places for them at the top schools remains unchanged. No wonder more and more parents push their kids to prepare for college practically before they are out of diapers. In high schools, students these days take on unprecedented loads of AP courses. (For the ambitious junior, three is common; for seniors, four is the new normal.) Even so, high school is too late to start training. "One of my daughter's classmates has a pilot's license," Judith Warner, author of *Perfect Madness: Motherhood in the Age of Anxiety*, writes. "Twelve-year-olds are taking calculus," she says. The tale of the stressed-out young couple scrambling to hire highly paid coaches and counselors to get their three-year-old into a super-selective Ivy-oriented private preschool has become a national joke.

Not that anybody is laughing—and those with least reason to laugh are the kids (and their parents) who, midway through high school, realize they haven't been ticking off all the right boxes, haven't been science fair winners, haven't published an up-and-coming blog, haven't been on the debate team, haven't been summer interns, haven't even gotten a pilot's license. The most terrifying admissions nightmare used to be waking up one morning to a significant shortfall in the college savings fund or finally admitting that, actually, you have no such fund. The cost of a college education certainly has not gone down (quite the contrary), but money alone, even if you have it, won't buy you admission to the Ivy League. These days, the *really* bad dream is feeling that you have simply arrived too late for the party, before you have even sent out a single application.

## LEAD YOURSELF TO EARLY SUCCESS

The Ivy League is a highly valued brand. Read on, and you will get what you need to emulate what Harvard, Yale, and successful organizations and companies have done for centuries. They all know—and you *should* know—that the right brand communicates value and does so immediately, as well as through the long term.

Personal branding involves a series of strategic choices, the very first of which is your choice of university or college. If you aspire to lead, brand yourself a leader by choosing an institution of the Ivy League brand, the elite brand, the 1 percent brand. It will not only be a great education, it will be a great validation. Building a personal brand is creating the identity by which you want the world to know you and your value.

## BACK GATEWAYS: THE ALTERNATIVES

*So you've chosen an institution of the Ivy League brand, the elite brand, the 1 percent brand.* But what if no such institution chooses *you*? Not only is this a very real possibility, it is by far the most likely outcome of your quest for admission.

This book is not about the "safety schools," the alternatives to the very best. It is about exercising personal leadership to find and create alternative *ways* of getting *into* the very best, even when you are turned away for whatever reason: economic, social, socioeconomic, academic, or the precious senior-year weeks you missed when you came down with mono.

The tools you will find in the pages that follow are both strategically inspirational, culled from some of the most successful leaders in history, *and* immediately practical and useful. When the traditional front gateway of a top-branded school is closed to you, we show you another way in.

Many of the nation's most prestigious institutions have *back gateways*. Most of these alternatives are virtually unknown and all but secret, while others are just very underused. But don't be misled or discouraged by any negative connotations the phrase "back gateway" may call to mind. Each back gateway alternative is 100 percent legitimate. After all, it would be difficult for even the most generous and well intentioned of the highly selective institutions to develop a single admissions policy that would guarantee equal opportunity for all applicants. Think of these back gateways as institutional policies intended to dramatically increase the odds of admission for eligible applicants. They are available to both economically disadvantaged students and to those who may not have gained admission through conventional means. Most importantly, think of the back gateways as opportunities to be seized by those who have decided to think and act more like CEOs than like victims.

## A SHIFT TO THE FIRST PERSON

Why do I feel compelled to share my back gateway secrets with you? Let me tell you about how I came to write this book.

In nearly every culture, people invariably fall into two broad categories: the upper class and the lower class, the "haves" and the "have-nots." I was a have-not, which, growing up in south Georgia, meant that I was what people dismissed as "white trash." Even as a child, I knew my family was uneducated, but I understood the value of learning. I was also keenly aware that for a member of a lower-class family, getting the kind of education that would raise you up was extremely difficult. My journey from victim of the socioeconomic status quo to leader of my own company began when I was invited to join the Cub Scouts. I was invited to join by a "have"—at least, he lived in a better part of town—who didn't care that others called me "white trash." He could see that I was a decent kid.

That was a big break for me, and after years of diligent work in the Scouts, it was my turn to claim Eagle Scout status—the pinnacle of scouting. I completed the required paperwork, and all I needed was the signature of our district Scout executive. I didn't think getting him to sign would be any big deal, and when I approached him he readily conceded that I had certainly met all the requirements. But he said he could never sign that paper, not for *someone like me*.

"C.W., you come from those kinds of people who can never become an Eagle Scout. You are just not Eagle Scout material. It doesn't matter what you do, just forget about getting it. It will never happen for you."

With just four short sentences, he slammed the gate shut on what was at the time my greatest goal in life.

I remember crying. Maybe I cried for a few days. Maybe even a week. But then I stopped crying, pulled myself together, and pulled out the official regulations governing the rise to Eagle Scout. I read them carefully for myself, word for word, and what I discovered was that the final necessary document could be signed *either* by the district Scout executive *or* by the chairman of the District Scout Council. So I paid a visit to the chairman.

He looked at the paper, and he looked at me.

"C.W., you deserve this. You are just the kind of boy we want for a leader in the Boy Scouts. I'll sign this form, and I'll see you at the Eagle Scout ceremony at First Methodist Church this coming Sunday."

Even as I walked to the front of that church on the appointed day, I knew that I had just learned a lesson in leadership and determination. It was this: Just because one man refuses to open one gate, it doesn't mean you can't look for another man and another gate. When I walked to the front of that church, I felt prepared not only to be an Eagle Scout, but also to confront, master, and enjoy whatever challenges lay ahead of me.

I learned right then and there that the very first thing a leader has to do is lead himself, and that means setting goals. Making Eagle Scout had been my first goal. Now, evolving from poor white boy to poor young adult, I developed a new goal in life: to attend college.

Somehow, I talked myself into believing that a necessary first step toward this goal was to buy a car so I could leave Georgia and drive off to a university located far away. So the summer before I turned sixteen, I hitched a ride to Eden, Ontario, Canada, to work as a laborer in the tobacco fields and earn enough to buy a car. Each day after work, I would take a cold shower, but the tobacco tar never came off my skin, no matter how much soap I used or how hard I scrubbed. It wasn't long before I came down with nicotine poisoning. It nearly killed me, but I still went to work in the fields every day.

I was learning that the upward journey involves obstacles that can be overcome by merit and hard work, but I was also learning that success is largely a matter of where you are from, not who you are. As Malcolm Gladwell observed in his *Outliers* (2008), "People don't rise from nothing. . . . It makes a difference where and when we grew up. . . . It's not enough to ask what successful people are like. . . . It is only by asking where they are *from* that we can unravel the logic behind who succeeds and who doesn't."

Where you're from can damage you and hold you back, or it can make you all the more determined to rise. Me? I bought a shiny white car and drove off to college, where I took up residence in a rented trailer. No longer "white trash," I had become "trailer trash." And that meant I had come far, but I still had a long way to go. The college I enrolled in was not some distant institution, but the University of Georgia. I was wrong about having to drive far away to get an education. I learned a lot, especially from university vice president J. W. Fanning, a former farm boy who had once worked in my hometown and for whom the university's esteemed Fanning Institute was named. And what I learned helped equip me to become executive editor of *Ivy League Week*, *Education Letter*, and *Education Business Weekly*, and to become CEO of their parent company. My experiences there helped me in creating my business Open the Gates, an educational research firm designed to guide students in drawing up a Plan B to enter the Ivy League or other elite colleges.

For people who start out higher, for boys and girls who grow up with the benefits of wealth and connections, the odds of achieving political, economic, and social leadership are far better. Though in the case of the Ivy League, with its 90 percent rejection rate, the odds are still long, even for young adults of privilege.

These are facts of life. But just because they are facts doesn't mean they can't be manipulated, shaped, and molded to enable almost anyone to emerge from a world of missed opportunities as a leader.

This book is the key to the back gateways of seven universities of the Ivy League: Harvard, Yale, Columbia, Cornell, Dartmouth, Pennsylvania (Penn), and Brown (Princeton is not included in this book because it does not have a back gateway). These are the American universities with the most stringent application processes, strict eligibility requirements, and highest costs. Also in this book you will find the UK's "Oxbridge" colleges, Oxford and Cambridge. In addition, a "second tier" of universities, including the Massachusetts Institute of Technology (MIT), Duke University, Northwestern University, and the University of Virginia, have highly selective admission requirements and confer social and economic benefits on par with the traditional Ivy League. Gain admission to any of these institutions, and you will receive a first-class education, the promise of an impressive résumé, and career-enhancing membership in a tightly woven network of alumni relations. Earn a diploma from the Ivy League or those "second-tier" schools closely associated with it, and you are afforded enhanced opportunities to emerge as a leader in a variety of professional fields—most notably, in commerce, finance, and politics.

As Lynn O'Shaughnessy explains in "College Planning Mythbusters," the most elite schools "are eager to burnish their names or protect their already stellar reputations." They believe that one way to do this is "by rejecting even more applicants than in previous years." Rankings by respected authorities such as *U.S. News & World Report* "reward colleges that achieve and maintain high rejection rates." Increasingly, the traditionally standoffish schools of the Ivy League purposely "send out literature to candidates who don't measure up to their standards." Thrilled by these invitations, more and more high school seniors apply—without realizing, of course, that they have been invited not to enroll but to inch the school's ranking just a bit higher. The truth is, they never have a chance.

If you dream of an Ivy League education but can't afford it or don't think you have everything necessary to get in, or have already had the front gate slammed in your face, the solution is self-evident. It is *important* because it is *important to you.*

## HOW TO USE THIS BOOK

This book is for families and students who believe an Ivy League or other elite national college education is preferable to that of some other category of college. *If you are not convinced that you are a match for an Ivy League or elite national university, this book is not for you.* An Ivy League or other elite national college education is not the best fit for everyone. If, however, you have already made the decision that a "most selective" college education is what you want to pursue, then this is exactly the book you need.

I wrote this book for families and students—of any age—who have their sights set on gaining admission to a top-ranked college and are unwavering in their commitment to *get in*, even if they have already been told to *stay out*. I wrote this book for those who are determined to make their academic dreams come true.

You are about to discover a series of back gateways and hidden pathways that lead to the most highly selective universities in the world. I believe that by guiding you to these gateways and pathways, I will help you in your pursuit of knowledge and your quest for upward mobility. I also believe that this guidance will contribute to the emergence and success of future leaders.

You deserve a fair shot at a diploma from your school of choice—your "dream school," not your "safety." One route is through the back gateways that lead to the campuses of the Top 40 ranked schools. Here is your key.

## USING YOUR KEY

Throughout this book, you will find a wealth of information about some of the best universities in the world, ranging from detailed descriptions of academic programs and faculty-to-student ratios to historical facts and fun things to do on campus. I have also included an informative "Keybox" at the beginning of each chapter, which will give you an at-a-glance snapshot of each school, what it has to offer, and what is expected of those applying for admission.

Since our focus is on back gateways, I have assessed the degree of openness of each back gateway. Some are wide open, others half-open, and some just barely cracked ajar. These assessments are based on a variety of factors, the most important of which are annual admissions rates, program expectations, and the depth and breadth of application criteria and requirements.

Also within the Keybox you will find a rating of the cost of each back gateway as compared to the front gateway. Often—but not always—the back gateway costs significantly less than the conventional front-gate admission. Since an education has a price tag, it makes sense to get an idea of your likely return on investment, so you will also find the median starting salary for graduates.

Any students mentioned in this book by first name only are not real, but are composites based on real students whose information was provided to me by themselves or their colleges. Those mentioned with first *and* last names are all real.

That's it. The book is easy to use, and the keys are in your hand. We have a choice. We can wait for elite colleges to find the will and way to enroll students from low- or middle-income families, or families who simply "failed" to give their kids the "right" start when they were four years old. Or we can do what I did when I so badly wanted to be an Eagle Scout. We can find a different way in.

As Joseph A. Soares argued in *The Power of Privilege: Yale and America's Elite Colleges*, "We want [America] to be a land of opportunity where individuals can make of themselves what they will. We like competition but believe it should be meritocratic; the contest should be honest with outcomes that are just. Americans believe in education as the best way to sustain a meritocratic society. There is hardly anyone who does not want every youth to have the opportunity to attend good schools in the pursuit of academic excellence. Yet we have managed not to notice that our most prestigious colleges and universities are beyond the reach of most youths other than those from families in the top income percentile. . . . It was not supposed to work like that."

No, it *is* not supposed to work like that, and I have written this book to show you how it doesn't *have* to work like that. In addition, my blog at www.openthegates.com will keep you current with the latest research and info on all of the topics covered in this book, and there you can sign up for free updates about college admissions and back gateways into top colleges.

Come on around to the back gateway, and meet your Plan B.

—C. W. Henderson,
New Haven, Connecticut, 2013
cw@openthegates.com

# 1

# Welcome to Plan B

### ■ WHO IS THIS BOOK FOR?

1. Students who want to be Ivy League/Top 40 graduates
2. Students who didn't get in the first time
3. Students who were told they weren't "Ivy League material" (but are sure they are)
4. Students who lack the finances for an elite college education
5. Students who want an elite education at a discounted price
6. Kids whose parents didn't create "the perfect student"
7. Adults who want to go back for a second (or first) degree
8. Students of all ages and backgrounds who believe the value of Ivy League/Top 40 schools is in the quality of instructors and curriculum
9. Students who appreciate and desire the benefits of an elite alumni network
10. Students who don't mind "taking their time" to earn a bachelor's degree

## PLAN B

The afternoon was warm and bright with anticipation as William, a seventeen-year-old high school senior, nervously fingered the shiny green door of the mailbox beside his family's tidy driveway. He pulled it open, and the sight of the slim but heavy envelope embossed with the crimson-and-gold seal of Harvard University set his heart racing.

"VERITAS" was the simple motto on a shield wreathed by laurel: *TRUTH*.

For William, this *was* the moment of truth. An honors student with a 3.9 GPA, a fistful of glittering letters of recommendation, and killer SAT scores, he was a star athlete and senior class president. Sure, Harvard was his dream school. But why should he be nervous? If *he* couldn't walk through the front gate of Harvard Yard, who could?

William did not bother to remove the other letters from the mailbox. Holding the crisp envelope with the fingers of both hands, he didn't even flip the mailbox door back up. Instead, restraining himself as best he could, he gingerly tore open the envelope at the end where the stamp was, taking care not to rip the letter inside. Pressing the top and bottom of the envelope between the thumb and fingers of his left hand, he drew the letter out with his right and spread it open in the spring sunlight.

It was a brief paragraph, and William did not have to read it all. The first two words, "We regret," said everything, and they said it with the terrible finality of a hanging judge pronouncing sentence.

Through welling tears, William struggled to coax his unbelieving brain into thought. *What next? What's the next move? What's my "Plan B"?*

And then it came to him. There *was* no Plan B.


## SHATTERED DREAMS OF THE IVY LEAGUE

For those who have endured the frustration of playing the admissions game, there is one consolation: It is far more difficult to gain admission to the top universities, especially the Ivy League, than it is to actually excel as a student and graduate from one of these schools. For those obviously qualified but nevertheless excluded, as well as for those who may not quite qualify on paper (but nevertheless have the initiative to thrive in these academic institutions), the conventional admissions process is a dead end. A slipup in academic work, an unexceptional SAT score, or less than optimal finances are just a few of the factors that can disqualify an otherwise deserving candidate.

But even those, like William, who *are* academic stars often find themselves on the outside looking in. It is impossible to imagine how many great minds have abandoned the pursuit of a first-class education because the admissions process was far too daunting. They expect lofty academic requirements, but, in a growing trend, admission is being denied to applicants who not only meet the criteria, but seemingly embody all of the desirable qualities an Ivy League student should possess.

## THE IVY LEAGUE BRAND

There is no disputing that in today's increasingly aggressive working world it is nearly impossible to build a career or even get something more than a minimum wage job without a college degree. Less universally understood is the fact that *where* you spend all those days studying plays a huge role in determining where, how, and on just how much you will make your living. Let's nip any debate in the bud right here. Earning a diploma from a Top 40 school gives you a significant, sometimes even a dramatic, edge over everyone who earns a diploma elsewhere.

- Most employers immediately recognize the "brand names" of the top universities, so that a degree from one of them makes your résumé stand out above the rest.
- An Ivy League or other elite education gives you access to exclusive alumni associations and networks that can prove invaluable to your short- and long-term career pursuits.
- Ivy League alumni bonds are especially strong and enduring. Built on a venerable "old boy network," they form a system in which powerful alumni tend to recruit new graduates from their

cherished alma mater to fill top positions in the organizations they control.

Even colleges and universities below the Top 40 bow to the ivy-fringed campuses, recruiting their graduates for their own law, medical, and business schools, as well as for academic and research positions.

## BACK GATEWAY: HALF-PRICE ADMISSION

Earning an Ivy League or other Top 40 diploma is a life-changing event. Not the least of the changes is the boost to your earning power that comes with an elite degree. The trouble is that four (or more—keep reading) years at any elite school is likely to leave you with a mountain of debt that can bury all that extra earning power for years to come.

According to a sobering 2009 College Board study, an eighteen-year-old student who borrows the full amount of tuition and fees to attend a *public* university will be thirty-three before he or she earns out—that is, before earnings catch up with the total education debt owed. Borrow to attend a *private* university, and it will take even longer to pay off the debt. The Project on Student Debt (http://projectonstudentdebt.org /files/File/Debt_Facts_and_Sources.pdf) estimated that in 2008 the average graduate from a public university had $20,200 in student loan debt, whereas a graduate from a private nonprofit university (which includes the Ivy League and many of the other Top 40 schools) shouldered a debt of $27,650. The organization also reported that, again in 2008, 62 percent of graduates from public universities had student loan debt versus 72 percent of those graduating from nonprofit private institutions. Additionally, according to FinAid (www.finaid.org/loans), 13.5 percent of parents borrowed federally subsidized PLUS Loans in 2007–2008 to supplement their children's loans, incurring a debt averaging $23,298 after four years.

All of the figures given above assume the "traditional" four-year baccalaureate. However, five- and even six-year undergraduate careers are the norm these days. Only about 48 percent of students attending private colleges or universities graduate in four years. In public universities, the proportion is an appalling 27 percent. The chances are better than fifty-fifty that you or your family will be paying for more than four years of college.

## THE BACK GATEWAY DISCOUNT

As you will discover in the chapters that follow, entering by the back gateways of any of ten of the institutions in this book will save you significant tuition costs of 50 percent or more.

At Northwestern University, tuition through the back gateway, the School of Continuing Studies, is $1,320 per credit hour—compared to around $3,000 per credit hour for "traditional" students. You will still get a great education for less than half the price. Harvard University, the crown prince of the Ivy League, also offers students a chance to earn a Harvard degree for about 50 percent off via its back gateway, the Harvard University Extension School.

But even at institutions in which admission via the back gateway is no cheaper than it is through the front door, the alternative can still save you significant money in the long run. The reason is that most of the back gateway programs are more flexible than the traditional programs. They are designed to accommodate the more demanding work and travel schedules of students from all generations and backgrounds.

## FINDING THE BACK GATEWAY

Let's be careful to explain just what a back gateway is and how you go about finding it.

Simply put, the back gateway is an alternative method of gaining admission to your school of choice. The entrance process may involve taking certain courses at a different institution, completing course work in a "sister" program, or enrolling in a "direct transfer" curriculum at a junior college. What all back gateways have in common, however, is that they almost always take you to the same degree with the same diploma that the front entrance leads to.

It may surprise you to learn that nearly half of the top colleges in the United States, including half of the Ivy League, not only have a back gateway, but they leave it wide open. Nevertheless, most students have no idea how to access it. Before this book, no single source published the details of the back gateway alternative.

## AN ISSUE OF FAIRNESS

Remember, the back gateway is not some bogus way of sneaking into the Ivy League. All of the alternatives profiled here are 100 percent legitimate, and they are fair. In fact, the very foundation of the back gateway process rests entirely upon the concepts of equity and fairness. The back gateways are academic opportunities available to students unable to access these schools through the front gateway.

Think of the back gateway as an alternative strategy that levels the playing field.

It is for anyone who wants—earnestly, passionately—to get in.

## ASKING FOR DIRECTIONS

Providing alternative access into such coveted, highly selective universities as Harvard and Penn presents a fresh means of achieving the very highest academic success. The back gateway enhances the pursuit of knowledge, supports upward mobility, and ultimately contributes to the emergence and success of scholars from diverse backgrounds. The nation's leading educators and graduates have long known that there is a powerful relationship between academic opportunity and future success. They also have long been aware that many deserving students have been denied the chance to fully achieve personal and professional goals simply because they couldn't get into an elite university.

Don't give up hope. Getting from the back gateway to your degree may take some extra time and additional hard work, but if you are up for the challenge, the course is there for you to navigate. This book will draw you the maps you need to start your journey to those back gateways, and will present you with the set of keys you need to open them.

## BACK GATEWAY OVERVIEW

| School | Location | Gate Position | SAT | Housing | Minimum Age | Application Criteria |
|---|---|---|---|---|---|---|
| Harvard | Cambridge, MA | Wide open | No | Limited | <18 | Moderate |
| Penn | Philadelphia, PA | Wide open | No | Limited | 18 | Moderate |
| Columbia | New York, NY | Half-open | Yes | Limited | 19 | Moderate |
| Cornell | Ithaca, NY | Wide open | No | Limited | 18 | Moderate |
| Yale | New Haven, CT | Ajar | Recommended | None | 18 | Moderate |
| Brown | Providence, RI | Ajar | Yes | Limited | 20 | Moderate/High |
| Dartmouth | Hanover, NH | Half-open | Yes | None | 18 | Moderate |
| Oxford | Oxford, UK | Wide open | No | Yes | <18 | Moderate/High |
| Cambridge | Cambridge, UK | Wide open | No | Yes | <18 | Moderate/High |
| MIT | Cambridge, MA | Ajar | Yes | Yes | 18/24 | High |
| Emory | Atlanta, GA | Wide open | Yes | Yes | 18 | Moderate |
| Washington | St. Louis, MO | Wide open | Usually | Limited | 18 | Moderate |
| Duke | Durham, NC | Half-open | No | Yes | 18 | Moderate |
| CalTech | Pasadena, CA | Ajar | No | Yes | 18 | High |
| Northwestern | Evanston, IL | Wide open | No | None | 18 | Moderate |
| UVA | Charlottesville, VA | Varies | No | Varies | 20 | Moderate |
| Georgetown | Washington, DC | Wide open | No | Limited | 18 | Moderate |
| UW-Madison | Madison, WI | Wide open | Varies | Yes | <18 | Moderate |
| NYU | New York, NY | Wide open | No | Yes | 19 | Moderate |
| USC | Los Angeles, CA | Half-open | No | Yes | 18 | Moderate |
| Boston College | Boston, MA | Wide open | No | Limited | <18 | Moderate |
| W&M | Williamsburg, VA | Wide open | Yes | Yes | 18 | Moderate |
| Georgia Tech | Atlanta, GA | Half-open | No | Yes | 18 | Moderate/High |
| UC Berkeley | Berkeley, CA | Half-open | No | Limited | 18 | Moderate |
| Notre Dame | South Bend, IN | Ajar | Yes | Limited | 18 | Moderate |

# 2

# Hello, Harvard

---

**KEYBOX**

SCHOOL: Harvard University

LOCATION: Cambridge, Massachusetts

COLLEGE RANKING: 1

GATE POSITION: Wide open

SAT REQUIRED: No

HOUSING: Limited

MINIMUM AGE (FOR GATEWAY APPLICANTS): 18 (or younger with parental consent)

APPLICATION CRITERIA: Moderate

MEDIAN STARTING SALARY: $60,000

COST COMPARED TO FRONT GATEWAY: Half

---

Sarah's Harvard dreams began when she was still a little girl. She had always liked school, and people told her that Harvard was the very best school in America, maybe even in the world. All through elementary and middle school, she kept dreaming, and the dream grew even more vivid when she entered high school. She was a model student, maintaining an impressive 3.8 grade point average, taking all the honors and AP courses her school offered, making herself active in student government, and even earning a spot as cocaptain of the varsity girls' soccer team.

But then came the SATs.

She studied. She prepped. She practiced. And she was crushed when her combined score came out "only" in the nineteen hundreds. She tried again, and she tried again. But the digits refused to budge upward.

For Sarah, years of dreaming shattered against the hard wall of a set of numbers. Her high school counselor confirmed what she already knew. Her SATs weren't likely to get her so much as a passing nod from Harvard, so she didn't even try. Instead, she settled for a small liberal arts college close to her hometown.

Boredom set in fast. At the end of her freshman year, Sarah told her parents that she'd decided to "take some time off," but, actually, she was thinking to herself that maybe college just wasn't for her.

So she found a job—and a pitifully small paycheck—writing for a local newspaper. As she worked, she found her old dream of a Harvard diploma bubbling back to the surface. By this time, Sarah had learned enough about being a newspaper reporter to know that, sometimes, you have to dig deep for your story. She dug, and she turned up a college admissions researcher who told her about a back gateway to Harvard.

It had a name, an impressive, big-sounding name—Harvard University Extension School—yet no one else, including her high school guidance counselor, had ever mentioned it, and no one she talked to now had ever even heard of it.

Was it top secret? And did that secrecy mean it was really hard to get into?

No, and no.

Sarah found out that getting in required nothing more than signing up for a series of qualifying courses, fulfilling a set of course requirements, then applying for admission to the degree program of the Harvard University Extension School. There were no secrets and nothing to pass stealthily under the table. And those SATs? You didn't even have to take them.

## "THE PINNACLE OF POWER AND PRESTIGE"

One person's cherished dream may seem utterly insubstantial to another. That's the way it is with dreams. No one, however, could find a more substantial foundation to build a dream on than Harvard University.

The first institution of higher learning established in America, Harvard was founded in 1636 and for most of its existence has enjoyed an unparalleled reputation for academic excellence, social influence, and financial privilege. As the *Boston Globe* recently put it, "By nearly every measure, Harvard stands at the pinnacle of power and prestige."

Physically, the school is precisely what the phrase *Ivy League* conjures. Sited over seven square miles of stately Cambridge, Massachusetts, the campus consists of venerable lecture halls (ivy-encrusted, naturally), sleek research facilities, and cozy dormitories ("houses," they are called in British university fashion) that have produced some of the world's most prominent leaders and renowned scholars.

Known humbly at its founding as "New College" and "College at New Towne," the university was officially named Harvard College in 1639 to honor a clergyman, John Harvard, who died young—at thirty-one—in 1638 and left to New College more than half of his estate, including four hundred books that are the nucleus of what is today a fifteen-million-volume library, the largest academic library in the world.

By the early 1900s, Harvard came to be regarded as the model the nation's other universities were to emulate, and today it is unquestionably the institution against which all schools that aspire to excellence are measured and, indeed, measure themselves.

## ONE TOUGH TICKET TO GET

If institutions that strive to be the best look to Harvard for a model, students who aim to graduate from the best apply to Harvard. For the vast majority of these students, the aspiration will remain just that—an aspiration, unfulfilled. Harvard has long had the lowest acceptance rate in the country, and in fall 2011 was at the lowest in the history of the university: 6.3 percent. By January 2012, 34,302 students were applying, of which a mere 2,032 received acceptance letters.

Based on the figures for 2012, the likelihood of receiving a painful rejection as a result of applying to Harvard University is about 94 percent. Nevertheless, it is a certainty that thousands of applications will continue to jam the mailbox of the Harvard Admissions Office year after year. It's not that legions of graduating high schoolers are closet masochists, but that legions of young men and women are thoroughly convinced that a Harvard degree is *the* golden ticket to a full and prosperous life.

Harvard sends a message of academic excellence to students and educators that adds to the urgency as well as the challenge of "getting in." That "golden ticket" is one tough ticket to get. But if you are ready to take on Harvard University, then consider taking the back gateway through Harvard University Extension School.

## TWO NAMES, ONE DIPLOMA

Harvard University Extension School and Harvard College are two separate schools within Harvard University. Harvard College is the principal undergraduate school of Harvard University, whereas Harvard University Extension School was designed to accommodate working adults, or students with academic needs that differ from those enrolled in the "traditional" program. According to the Extension School, its program is designed for part-time students and offers flexible evening, summer, and online courses. Many students are adults, but eighteen is the minimum age for admission without parental permission (younger applicants require a signature), and whether you are eighteen, twenty-eight, fifty-eight, or older, you will find a curriculum that accommodates and complements an active life. Moreover, students at the Harvard University Extension School exhibit a diversity in age, background, and life experience beyond what is typically found at Harvard College. This creates an intellectually rich learning environment, setting the stage for graduate school admission and a rewarding career.

The school offers a wide range of courses in more than sixty-five fields of study, from anthropology and linguistics to biology and computer science. The total absence of progress requirements and prescribed deadlines for graduation makes the program ideal for part-time students and those who want to take their time earning a degree.

## ACCREDITATION AND DEGREES OFFERED

Harvard University Extension School is accredited by the New England Association of Schools and Colleges, and its curriculum is approved each year by Harvard's Faculty of Arts and Sciences to count toward a bachelor of liberal arts (A.L.B.) or a master of liberal arts (A.L.M.) degree. (We will consider only the undergraduate degree here.)

Students can earn an A.L.B. in one of three areas of concentration: the humanities, sciences, or social sciences. Within their chosen area of concentration, students may pursue one of twenty "focused fields of study," including:

Anthropology and archaeology

Biology

Computer science

Creative writing

Dramatic arts

Economics

English

Environmental studies

French

Government

History

International relations

Journalism

Literature

Mathematics

Philosophy and ethics

Psychology

Religion

Spanish

Visual arts

## YES, THIS IS THE REAL HARVARD UNIVERSITY

Since 1909, more than thirteen thousand students have been awarded degrees and certificates from Harvard University Extension School, with an average of one hundred degree recipients a year. Yes, this is the *real* Harvard University, which has only two schools that grant undergraduate degrees. One, Harvard College, you enter through the front gateway. The other, Harvard University Extension School, can be accessed through the back. Despite the different portals, both issue bona fide Harvard University diplomas. Earn an A.L.B., and you'll be awarded a diploma inscribed with this language:

HARVARD UNIVERSITY...

*The President and Fellows of Harvard College...*

*Degree of Bachelor of Liberal Arts in Extension Studies*

Note that, while the program is administered by the Extension School, the degree itself is awarded by the President and Fellows of *Harvard College.* Moreover, the program is called the Bachelor of Liberal Arts Program, and the faculty of the Harvard University Extension School refers to the diploma as the Bachelor of Liberal Arts diploma. Although the diploma document does say "Extension Studies" as part of the degree, it makes no reference to the "Extension School." Thus, earn a diploma through study at the Harvard University Extension School, and the outside world will recognize you as the holder of a *Harvard* diploma. Period. And not just the *outside* world. Harvard University Extension School graduates are welcome to toss their mortarboards along with everyone else at the Harvard Yard commencement.

If you still need more perspective, look at it this way: Harvard University Extension School is one of fourteen schools at Harvard University. The thirteen others are Business, Dental Medicine, Design, Divinity, Education, Engineering, Government, Graduate School of Arts and Sciences, Harvard College, Law, Medicine, Public Health, and the Radcliffe Institute for Advanced Studies. Of these schools, only Harvard College and Harvard University Extension School offer undergraduate degrees.

## GETTING TO THE BACK GATEWAY

Earning a degree through the Extension School does have its fair share of requirements. Let's start with the easiest ones.

To take courses at Harvard Extension School, you register. No other application is required—until you decide to pursue a degree.

To register, you will need to provide your name and address, either a telephone number or an email address, and you must be proficient in English. You'll need a copy of the college catalogue, either in print or online, so that you can select your courses and complete a registration form. If you're younger than eighteen, you'll need a parent's or guardian's authorization to enroll. You don't have to furnish high school transcripts or, for that matter, a social security number. You will, however, need some money: typically $995 to $1,950 (payable by check or credit card) for each course you take.

Put all of this in the mail, and you are enrolled at Harvard!

Should you ever not believe that you are really enrolled at Harvard, you can request an official "Letter of Enrollment" from the university for the current term. This document will include your name, student ID number, term dates, and course information. It is embossed and signed by the registrar, and it is free of charge. You may obtain as many copies as you want, and they can be sent to friends, relatives, employers, other third parties, or to you directly.

## CROSSING THE THRESHOLD

So you've made it into the Ivy League, yes?

Yes—and also not quite.

You are *enrolled*, but you have not been *admitted* into a Harvard undergraduate degree program. You have found the back gateway to Harvard, and you are at the threshold. You still have to cross.

Now that you are enrolled, the next step toward a Harvard degree requires following the back gateway all the way to the front door. While Harvard Extension School has no real requirements for enrollment, it does require you to take very specific actions for admission to the degree program.

After enrolling in a course or courses, you will have to make some important decisions:

Do you want to enroll in accelerated (often referred to as "experimental") three-week classes?

Do you want to take advantage of distance education and online options?

Is summer school for you?

Do you want to enroll in night school?

After choosing among these options—and you *can* mix and match—you must now actually take a few courses and make good grades to demonstrate that you are ready for admission to a degree program.

Regardless of the form of study you have chosen, whether accelerated classes, distance education, summer school, night school, or some combination of these, in order to get into a degree program, you will have to earn B– grades or higher in three undergraduate-level courses or four-credit liberal arts courses from the degree program of your choice. These courses are more than just prerequisites for admission into the degree program. They will also count as twelve program credits toward graduation once you are admitted.

## REALITY CHECK

You've acted on your Ivy League dream, and that's great, but before you get lost in fantasies of Commencement Day, understand that you really do have to work hard to earn that diploma. Harvard course work is demanding. The Harvard University Extension School may seem like an "easy" way to get into Harvard, and it certainly does present far fewer obstacles to entry than the traditional front gateway. But the reality is this: You will still have to apply yourself. The Harvard University Extension School Catalogue puts it this way: "Given that 35 is the average age of our students, SAT scores and high school grades are not relevant predictors of success. Your ability to do honors-level work at Harvard is the most relevant predictor." In other words, at the Harvard Extension School, you are presumed capable, and the gateway is open to you. Once inside, it is up to you to prove that presumption with actual performance. You've been given a chance, not a free pass.

## WRITE YOURSELF IN

In addition to proving yourself by earning B– or better grades in three undergraduate-level courses, you, as a degree candidate, must also pass an intensive writing course called Expository Writing (EXPO E-25, or EXPO S-20 for the summer school version), also with a B– or better.

Expository Writing is often referred to by Extension School insiders as the "gatekeeper course" because it will determine whether you are prepared for the intensive and demanding curriculum of Harvard University Extension School. According to the university, the Expository Writing course is designed to teach the core skills of academic writing, including analysis, argument, and the proper use of sources.

After earning a B– or better in three undergraduate courses plus Expository Writing, you are free to move on to the next step toward admission to a degree program. This is a two-page, double-spaced application essay, which must be deemed "satisfactory" by the Admissions Committee.

It's no secret that the committee likes first-person narrative, so get ready to write about yourself in your own voice. The school provides helpful writing directions for the essay, called "Guidelines for Good Academic Writing," which will walk you step-by-step through your essay. The document even furnishes an instructive list of reasons why the Admissions Committee might return an essay for revisions—which means, by the way, that the committee doesn't reject essays out of hand. "If your essay does not meet the Committee's expectations," the catalogue explains, "you will have an opportunity to revise it." Not only is the back gateway a second chance for aspiring Ivy Leaguers, the attitude in the Extension School Admissions Committee, though demanding, is decidedly more welcoming than exclusionary. If necessary, an undergraduate advisor will even pick up the phone and call you with suggestions on how to improve your application essay.

Among the topics you can select for your essay are the impact on your life of the Extension School's courses taken to date; why you want a degree from the Extension School; and how a liberal arts education will contribute to your personal or professional growth.

## BUILD ON WHAT YOU HAVE

In a program so welcoming, there is one significant exclusion. To be eligible to apply for a degree, you must not already possess one. This does not mean, however, that the Harvard University Extension School must be the first and only undergraduate institution you have attended. If you come to the school with some undergraduate work from another college, you'll need to obtain official transcripts for all previous course work, and you will have to prepare and submit a résumé with your application for admission into the degree program.

The Extension School is very flexible about allowing you to complete an undergraduate degree that you began elsewhere. It accepts transfer credits from fully accredited universities, as long as you passed with a grade of C– or higher. For that matter, this back gateway to Harvard University can also serve as an alternative to high school. As the catalogue explains, "The Harvard Extension School is sufficiently flexible to be the 'right' program for people of all ages, academic backgrounds, and current circumstances. Accelerated home-schooled students join the program as a more rigorous alternative to high school."

It is no wonder that students at the Extension School range in age from the early teens to well into the eighties. The average age of extension students is thirty-five with the majority of candidates for the A.L.B. at about age thirty-five. Most enter the program having completed about a year and a half of previous college work elsewhere. Students come from 118 countries and 46 states, and typically have a wealth of life and work experience. They may also have a lot of demands on their time, so many Harvard College lectures are recorded during regular class periods and podcast for Harvard Extension School distance-education courses, giving enrolled students the option to "attend" lectures entirely at their convenience.

## SEE YOU IN CLASS

After you have completed and submitted the application, your next assignment is to wait for word from the Admissions Committee. Receiving an acceptance letter means that you are not only officially registered, but also admitted as a degree candidate at Harvard University Extension School. Now all you have to do for your A.L.B. is complete 128 credits and maintain good academic standing, which means a 2.0 GPA. In other words, you have to *be* a Harvard undergraduate.

## HOUSING AND TUITION

Life for students who enter through the back gateway is not all that different from that of students who came through the front—with one significant exception. Although Extension School students reap the benefits of attending school in Cambridge, Boston's "Left Bank" celebrated for its thriving, diverse culture, its charming cafes, and stimulating bookstores, Extension students are on their own when it comes to housing. Harvard University Extension School was initially designed for a commuting student population, so it does not provide on-campus living accommodations. This said, students already registered in their prerequisite courses can obtain a rundown of housing opportunities in Cambridge and the surrounding area by visiting the Harvard Real Estate Housing Office. The office even maintains a roommates-wanted list.

Because the office does not respond to email, mail, or telephone inquiries, students must visit in person. It is located at 7 Holyoke Street and is open from 9 a.m. to 5 p.m. on Monday, Wednesday, Thursday, and Friday.

Note that if you are planning on attending Harvard Summer School, the situation is different. On-campus housing *is* available for summer school students.

The cost to attend Harvard University Extension School is significantly less than "traditional" tuition at Harvard University, with individual courses ranging from $995 to $1,950—and that's per course, not per credit—about half the cost of front gateway courses.

## STUDENT SERVICES

Harvard Extension School offers a variety of student services to admitted degree candidates, in addition to a number of special options and curriculum choices.

As in all other Harvard degree programs, student advising and preliminary degree advising are available. Additionally, once admitted to the degree program, registered certificate, degree, and diploma candidates are issued a Harvard student identification card that provides access to most of Harvard's on-campus resources and the facilities of the Athletic Department. Students are eligible for Harvard computer accounts (primarily for educational use), and they are granted full access to the magnificent Harvard libraries. Extension students can even purchase health insurance—including dental—by applying through the University Health Services.

## ALUMNI SERVICES AND THE IVY LEAGUE NETWORK

Remember, a degree from the Harvard Extension School is a degree from Harvard University. This means that graduates have the option of becoming full members of the Harvard Alumni Association, a membership that can be of great value in the work and professional world. In addition, as the catalogue explains, "career counseling services, including the OCS [Office of Career Services] referral option, can help students find their dream jobs." The catalogue promises that Extension School "graduates find that their degree enables them to advance within their current profession or change careers." You would not expect any less from Harvard University.

For more information, contact:

Harvard University
51 Brattle Street
Cambridge, MA 02138-3722
(617) 495-4024
Website: www.extension.harvard.edu
Email: extension@dcemail.harvard.edu

# 3

# Welcome to Penn

> ▪ **KEYBOX**
>
> **SCHOOL:** University of Pennsylvania
>
> **LOCATION:** Philadelphia, Pennsylvania
>
> **COLLEGE RANKING:** 8
>
> **GATE POSITION:** Wide open
>
> **SAT REQUIRED:** No
>
> **HOUSING:** Limited
>
> **MINIMUM AGE:** 18
>
> **APPLICATION CRITERIA:** Moderate
>
> **MEDIAN STARTING SALARY:** $60,400
>
> **COST COMPARED TO FRONT GATEWAY:** Half or less

After she graduated from high school, Lisa took a job as a waitress in a posh restaurant on Philadelphia's Main Line. For as long as she could remember, she had dreamed of attending college to pursue a degree in creative writing, but her family could not afford the cost of tuition. The tips were very good at the restaurant, however, and Lisa thought she might just be able to swing it on her own financially; however, it seemed impossible to shoehorn classes into her busy work schedule.

She was resigned to giving up college as a lost cause until, one evening shift, a coworker told her about a degree program that was absolutely perfect for working students. What's more, it was offered by one of the best schools in the nation: Penn, the University of Pennsylvania.

When Lisa finally walked through the back gateway opened by the College of Liberal and Professional Studies, she not only discovered an admissions process that was surprisingly straightforward, but she realized that she had entered a world of attentive professors who taught classes that were small enough to provide plenty of one-on-one instruction. Most surprising to her, she immediately felt that she fit in. Here was an Ivy League university that was anything but clubby and stuffy. The urban Philadelphia campus was diverse, affording her an opportunity to learn about cultures, traditions, and ideas that were new to her as she studied in the company of students of all ages and backgrounds.

She stayed on at the restaurant as she attended classes. When she accepted her diploma four years after enrolling, she was convinced that learning about the back gateway to Penn was the best tip anyone had ever given her.

## PENN THE INNOVATIVE

The University of Pennsylvania started out as a church for an eighteenth-century American evangelist superstar—Reverend George Whitefield—as well as a charity school. Fund-raising for the building, the biggest in colonial Philadelphia at the time, got under way in 1740. Although the contributors raised enough cash to begin construction, they fell short when it came to sustaining both Whitefield *and* the charity school. Unwilling to let the magnificent edifice go derelict and never one to pass up an opportunity for public service, Benjamin Franklin promoted the idea of creating a "Public Academy in Philadelphia." As he proposed it, the new institution would be a radical departure from higher education as it then existed in the colonies. Whereas Harvard, William & Mary, and Yale—the only three colonial colleges at the time—had all been founded primarily to prepare an educated clergy for America's Protestant churches, the new *public* academy would be totally secular. Instead of preparing clergy, it would prepare citizens, exposing them to a blend of liberal arts and practical learning designed to foster an attitude of enlightened public service even as it enabled them to earn a handsome living.

Both the idea and the institution caught on. In 1755, the Academy of Philadelphia was renamed the College of Philadelphia. In 1779, during the American Revolution, the state legislature separately created the University of the State of Pennsylvania. After independence had been won in 1791, the state granted a new charter, merging the College and the University into one as the University of Pennsylvania. To this day, Penn is often mistaken for a state school, but it was and remains a private, nonprofit university.

Situated on an idyllic, tree-lined campus along the Schuylkill River, bordering the bright lights of center-city Philadelphia, the university offers an extraordinary array of resources to approximately ten thousand undergraduate and ten thousand graduate students. It boasts a course catalogue the print version of which is as thick as a phone book.

With its lofty eighth-place standing in the 2013 *U.S. News & World Report* rankings of all universities and with fifteen Nobel Prize winners among its faculty and alumni, it is little wonder that the school's acceptance rate is a competitive 12.4 percent. An international center for interdisciplinary learning and research, the university is supported by a massive endowment of more than $6 billion.

The University of Pennsylvania is a great Ivy League institution with a slightly edgy urban identity. And while about eight out of ten applicants are turned away at the front gate, its back gate swings wide open.

## PENN'S BACK GATEWAY

The College of Liberal and Professional Studies (LPS), formerly known as the College of General Studies, was established to offer superb liberal arts and professional programs on a schedule accommodating to the busy lives of working students. As part of Penn's School of Arts and Sciences, LPS attracts what the college characterizes as "highly motivated and intellectually outstanding students" from age eighteen up. Once you are admitted to the LPS program, you will take the same courses as "traditional" students, whether during the day or in the evening, and you will earn full academic credit for them. Complete the course work successfully, and you will receive the same degree as traditional graduates.

There *are* three significant differences between LPS and the "regular" undergrad program.

First, LPS tuition is *less* than half the standard rate of front gateway tuition.

Second, LPS students generally must live off of campus; on-campus accommodations range from very limited to none, depending on space available after all the requirements of regular full-time students have been met.

Third, students under the age of twenty-one may only attend on a part-time basis.

## How to Apply

LPS operates on a rolling admissions schedule, which means that personnel review applications as soon as they are received instead of waiting for deadlines to pass. The application fee is $70, and according to LPS officials, applicants typically receive word of a decision within ten days of submitting their materials. Applications can be submitted online only, at www.sas.upenn.edu/lps/undergraduate/ba/application.

Admission requires a 3.0 cumulative GPA from high school graduates. Applicants who did not finish high school may apply if they have taken a high school equivalency exam or have scored at least 300 on the General Educational Development (GED) exam. Other than the GED, no other standardized tests, including the SAT, are required for admission. Nor does LPS require letters of recommendation; however, the Admissions Committee will accept and review any letters you may wish to supply. If you are certain that you can secure stellar recommendations, furnishing the letters can only help.

All applicants are required to write essays in response to four topics:

1. Have you ever been placed on probation, dismissed or suspended from any college or university for reasons pertaining to academic integrity? If yes, please include any facts that you believe bear on the significance of this circumstance.
2. Describe your educational history and background, making sure to address whether your records and transcripts accurately reflect your academic ability. Explain fully if you have ever withdrawn, taken a leave of absence, or been dropped by any school, college, or university.
3. Write a brief essay describing your academic and personal goals and explain how these will be furthered by study at Penn in general and at LPS in particular. Feel free to discuss a specific academic topic you have enjoyed studying and explain why it is of interest to you.
4. Describe any nonacademic experiences that you feel strengthen your application such as employment, travel, community affairs, volunteer work, publications, etc.

You will be instructed to upload your essays together in a single document at the LPS website. Their combined length should not exceed the equivalent of four typewritten double-spaced pages.

If you have been out of high school for an extended period of time, the admissions committee will give full weight to such aspects of background experience as your work, travel, community service, and volunteer activities. Depending on your academic record and other considerations, the committee may decide to grant admission on a provisional basis, to give you an opportunity to prove yourself by actually taking some LPS undergraduate courses. After you complete four courses with a cumulative grade point average of at least 2.7, your provisional status will be reevaluated for full admission.

LPS calls itself the "oldest lifelong learning program in the Ivy League." The adjective *lifelong* accurately suggests that the program is tailored to the needs of working students who are generally older than the traditional undergraduate. University officials counsel applicants under twenty-one, who are limited to taking no more than two courses per semester, to "consider carefully the differences between part-time study and a full-time residential college experience." LPS encourages interested students of all ages to meet with an academic advisor to discuss their plans. This can be done in person or over the telephone.

## AN ALTERNATIVE TO THE ALTERNATIVE

Although LPS is the main back gateway into Penn, there is another alternate entrance. You can find it on the campus of the Pennsylvania Academy of the Fine Arts (PAFA).

Founded in 1805 by two giants of early nineteenth-century American Art, painter Charles Willson Peale and sculptor William Rush, PAFA is the oldest arts institution in the United States. It has a rich and proud history at the forefront of the nation's fine arts education. PAFA enjoys international recognition for its collections of nineteenth- and twentieth-century paintings and sculpture, as well as more contemporary artwork. Among the masterpieces in the PAFA collection are works by such renowned American artists as Winslow Homer, Childe Hassam, and Robert Motherwell. PAFA graduates include the varied likes of painter Mary Cassatt, whose career spanned the late nineteenth and early twentieth centuries, and cutting-edge filmmaker David Lynch. In 2005, the Academy received the National Medal of the Arts for "extraordinary contributions to the creation, growth and support of the arts in the United States."

In 2008, nearly four hundred students attended PAFA, acquiring the fundamentals of drawing, painting, sculpture, and printmaking under the tutelage of more than sixty faculty members and visiting artists. If you are interested in a fine arts program, the PAFA-Penn connection may be just right for you.

PAFA offers a four-year certificate program, a post-baccalaureate program, a master's in fine arts (M.F.A.), and, in concert with the University of Pennsylvania, a bachelor of fine arts (B.F.A.) degree. The "Coordinated Bachelor of Fine Arts Program with the University of Pennsylvania" combines Penn's Ivy League academics with world-class training in the hands-on studio arts. If you are accepted into the program, you may either take Penn classes concurrently with PAFA studio courses, or you may choose to complete PAFA requirements before finishing the required Penn courses. You may apply for acceptance into the BFA program when you apply to PAFA or at any time during your enrollment in the PAFA "Certificate Program." Either way, as an Academy student, you are eligible to attend classes at Penn after you complete one year of academic work at PAFA.

To receive the degree, "Coordinated BFA students" must complete ninety credits of course work (three years of study) at PAFA and sixteen courses at the University of Pennsylvania. These include four required courses in art history and twelve elective courses at the School of Arts and Sciences. In addition, students have the option of completing a fourth year in PAFA's studio program. This not only allows them to spend an additional year in their private studio, but sends them into the world with both a University of Pennsylvania B.F.A. *and* a PAFA certificate. Finally, while studying at the University of Pennsylvania, students may also declare an academic minor. Usually, this requires completing six courses in the area of minor study.

Designed for maximum flexibility, the PAFA back gateway helps students earn a Penn diploma that will prepare them for careers in the field of fine arts, including work as museum curators, gallery professionals, and arts administrators, in addition to pursuing independent creative arts careers.

## How to Apply

The PAFA application fee is $70, but the Academy does have some stringent requirements for admission.

Academic records are carefully reviewed for admission. All application materials must be submitted in one envelope or package at the same time and must include:

1. The completed application
2. A portfolio containing work on digital media (CD, DVD, etc.), slides, or actual original work representing the student's art capabilities
3. A high school transcript or GED
4. Two letters of recommendation
5. Official TOEFL scores for nonnative speakers of English
6. A one- to two-page typed, double-spaced essay that, based on the strengths of what you might write, answers one, two, or all of the following questions:
   • What kind of an artistic environment are you looking for in a school?
   • How has art history influenced your work?
   • What is your favorite material, and why?

PAFA's website (www.pafa.org) offers a guide with step-by-step instructions for preparing application portfolios.

## HOUSING AND TUITION

According to the Penn website, LPS "has a commitment to keeping tuition costs down for part-time students and to making Penn more accessible to the Philadelphia community." Recognizing that financial aid is not always readily available to part-time students, LPS offers them lower tuition costs and specialized scholarships. In addition, LPS reduces costs by hiring professors from Penn and other schools to teach its courses rather than supporting its own complete and independent college departments. Detailed tuition schedules for individual programs are available on the school's website.

LPS students have very limited options for on-campus housing. If you desperately want to live on campus, you may contact the office of Housing and Conference Services to be placed on a waiting list. Fortunately, the neighborhood surrounding the University of Pennsylvania offers a rental market that is both thriving and reasonably priced. The school advises students to contact the Office of Off-Campus Living for assistance with finding housing.

If you choose to take the PAFA gateway, you will find absolutely no on-campus student housing available. This said, PAFA's Student Services Office will work with you to help you find suitable off-campus housing.

PAFA tuition is based on a nine-month academic year and varies from student to student. Check out the PAFA website to see the tuition schedule that applies to each program. "Please keep in mind," the website explains, "that here at PAFA we work very hard to keep our costs low and work hard to keep our educational experience within reach of all."

For more information, contact:

University of Pennsylvania
College of Liberal and Professional Studies
3440 Market Street, Suite 10
Philadelphia, PA 19104-3335
(215) 898-7326
Website: www.sas.upenn.edu/LPS/admissions
Email: LPS@sas.upenn.edu

Pennsylvania Academy of the Fine Arts
Coordinated Bachelor of Fine Arts Program
118–128 N. Broad Street
Philadelphia, PA 19102
(215) 972-7600
Website: www.pafa.org
Email: admissions@pafa.edu

# 4

## Ivy in the Apple:
## Columbia University

---

**KEYBOX**

SCHOOL: Columbia University

LOCATION: New York, New York

COLLEGE RANKING: 4

GATE POSITION: Half-open

SAT REQUIRED: Yes

HOUSING: Limited

MINIMUM AGE: 19

APPLICATION CRITERIA: Moderate

MEDIAN STARTING SALARY: $57,300

COST COMPARED TO FRONT GATEWAY: Same

---

"No question in the classroom was ever stupid," Jacques Pépin said of his student days at Columbia University's School of General Studies. Today a globally renowned celebrity chef, TV personality, and dean of Special Programs at New York's prestigious International Culinary Center, Chef Pépin already had a well-established career preparing sublime meals for the most discerning palates when he decided to enroll at Columbia in the early 1960s.

In 1959, he left Paris—where he had been personal chef to President Charles de Gaulle—and arrived in New York City with a limited command of the English language. He went to work full-time as a chef at the exclusive Le Pavillon while attending the School of General Studies (GS). After receiving his bachelor's degree, he later continued at Columbia's graduate school, earning a master's in eighteenth-century French literature in 1972. Today, this author of more than twenty cookbooks and frequent host of television cooking shows attributes his success in large measure to his experience at GS. Writing in the GS catalogue, he notes that "without an age limit for enrollment at GS, without a class system like in France, there was no shame in coming from a humble background or having a lack of formal education. . . . It was truly America as I had envisioned it."

Jacques Pépin was already headed for a promising career when he enrolled at GS, but he wasn't content with being defined narrowly by that career. And he wasn't about to let his beginner's English and lack of a college education stop him from broadening his cultural horizons. Columbia University's back gateway was his passage to a richer life and greater success than even he imagined.

## WORLD CLASS LIKE THE UPPER WEST SIDE

With 6,027 full-time undergraduates enrolled for 2012–2013, the 253-year-old university on the Upper West Side of Manhattan is one of the smallest institutions in the Ivy League, but its reputation is clearly world class. Columbia's professors have always been leaders in their fields, and more than seventy Nobel laureates are affiliated with the university. Its academic programs are universally regarded as cutting edge, challenging, and rigorous.

Columbia was established by the Church of England in 1754 as King's College. Like most early American colleges, King's was founded primarily to prepare an educated clergy for the colonies. Also like those other schools, it soon became far more famous for shaping the minds of the developing nation's great secular leaders. America's first treasury secretary, Alexander Hamilton; its first chief justice, John Jay; Louisiana Purchase negotiator Robert Livingston; and Erie Canal builder Gouverneur Morris were among the Founding Fathers educated at King's. More recent Columbia alumni include four U.S. presidents—Theodore Roosevelt, Franklin D. Roosevelt, Dwight D. Eisenhower, and Barack Obama—a roster of international presidents and prime ministers, including Giuliano Amato, twice prime minister of Italy; Hafizulla Amin, former prime minister and president of Afghanistan; Michael O'Leary, prime minister of Ireland; Mary Robinson, former Irish president; and Mikhail Saakashvili, leader of Georgia's "Rose Revolution" and its current president. The list goes on.

Columbia was fourth among the nation's universities in the 2013 *U.S. News & World Report* rankings. As such, it attracts a high caliber of students to its thirteen graduate and professional schools and three undergraduate schools. Its relatively modest size combined with its stratospheric reputation produces a razor-thin 7 percent acceptance rate from the more than eighteen thousand students who apply each year. Despite this selectivity, Columbia has one of the most diverse student populations in the Ivy League, and it offers some fifteen hundred courses in more than seventy majors. More than a quarter of Columbia's students come from urban areas, and its Upper Manhattan location is a real-world learning experience in itself.

## COLUMBIA'S BACK GATEWAY

An optimist, the cliché goes, sees the glass half-full rather than half-empty. But even the most optimistic of optimists would have a hard time interpreting a 93 percent empty glass as 7 percent full. If you are one of the vast majority barred from Columbia's front gateway, check out the School of General Studies.

GS provides students the opportunity to take the same courses from the same faculty for the same degree as any other Columbia University undergraduate. Columbia University's extension offerings were reorganized in 1947 as a separate undergraduate college, the School of General Studies, to meet the needs of GIs returning from World War II.

Today, GS offers bachelor of arts (B.A.) and bachelor of science (B.S.) degrees. Both degree tracks require students to satisfy core requirements in science, literature, humanities, and social sciences, and then to specialize in a major field of study. There are a dazzling seventy-six majors from which to choose, ranging from *A* (African studies) to *Y* (Yiddish studies). Those students who choose a science major graduate with a B.S. degree; everyone else earns a B.A.

## How to Apply

You may apply to GS at any time of the year, but there are deadlines. For fall and summer enrollment, the deadline is June 1, and for spring, November 1. There are also "early action" deadlines available: March 1 for fall, April 1 for summer, and October 1 for spring.

In contrast to the extension-type programs at other institutions profiled in this book, all applicants are admitted to the School of General Studies from day one as degree candidates. You may enroll as a full- or part-time student, and you may change your status from semester to semester, according to your needs. This makes GS a very flexible program.

You may apply online or on paper. Either way, you can go to www .gs.columbia.edu/applying-gs, where you will find a link to the online application and a downloadable PDF version. Alternatively, you can phone the Admissions Office at (212) 854-2772 to receive the application forms by mail.

In addition to the completed application, you will have to submit:

1. Official high school transcripts, secondary school records, or GED test results. If you have a GED in addition to two or more years of high school, you will have to submit the transcripts as well as the GED test results.

2. Official transcripts from all colleges or universities attended. GS accepts up to sixty credits for work satisfactorily completed at other accredited institutions.

3. Official scores from either the Scholastic Assessment Test (SAT) or the American College Testing Program (ACT) taken within the last eight years. If you do not have SAT or ACT scores—or if your scores are older than eight years—you may instead take the General Studies Admissions Examination (GSAE) for a $25 fee.

4. A typed, double-spaced autobiographical essay of between 1,500 and 2,000 words. The admissions committee asks you to write "about your educational history, work experience, present situation, and plans for the future" and to "make sure to address why you consider yourself a nontraditional student and have chosen to pursue your education at the School of General Studies of Columbia University." The committee specifies that the essay "should not only identify and describe specific elements of the program, academic or otherwise, that meet your needs as a nontraditional student, but should also explain why GS is the place for you." You are invited to "attach one additional page to tell us anything else you would like us to know about you."

5. Two letters of recommendation from academic and/or professional sources.

6. A $75 application fee.

GS highly recommends submitting an application for scholarship along with the admissions application. Although the GS back gateway offers no tuition discount, scholarships and financial aid are available, and the administration urges prospective students to apply for them.

The Admissions Committee processes each application when it is complete, and admission decisions are made on a rolling basis, typically within four to six weeks of receiving a complete application. Applicants for the summer and fall terms are notified on a rolling basis through

July 15, while applicants for the spring term are notified through December 15. You can track the progress and status of your application online.

## QUALIFYING FOR A DEGREE

Remember, you are admitted to GS as a matriculated degree student, which entitles you to do course work that satisfies core requirements in science, literature, humanities, and social sciences plus courses toward the major of your choice. You will need to complete a total of 124 credits with a minimum grade point average of 2.0. The credits are distributed among GS core requirements, major requirements, and electives. All GS students must complete a major in order to graduate.

## GS STUDENT PROFILE

In 2010, GS reported thirteen hundred students enrolled, with a median age of twenty-nine. Of these, 60 percent were full-time and 40 percent part-time. The 2010 student body was typically diverse, evenly divided by gender, with 29 percent of the American students Asian-American, African-American, Hispanic/Latino, or Native American. Seventeen percent of the student body was from outside the United States, representing a total of sixty-four countries.

As mentioned, GS students are free to change their status from full-time to part-time on a semester-to-semester basis. Do note that there are some perks for switching to full-time status. Only full-time GS students are eligible for university housing—a significant benefit in a city notorious for high housing costs.

## ALTERNATIVE GATEWAYS

Like Penn, Columbia University has more than one back gateway. There are at least three, possibly four. Although the alternative back gateways are considerably more exclusive than entering via GS, they may be just right for you.

*Alternative 1.* Students can earn a dual degree through the Joint Program of the School of General Studies and the Albert A. List College of the Jewish Theological Seminary (JTS). This program combines traditional liberal arts with intensive Jewish Studies, offering bachelor's degrees from both JTS and GS. Students in the program take a full spectrum of courses in the Bible, Hebrew language, Jewish history, Jewish literature, Jewish philosophy, Talmud, and rabbinics, while receiving a superior liberal arts education. While some graduates of the program choose ordination or other careers in the Jewish community, many students pursue a wide variety of other professions.

*Alternative 2.* The second alternative back gateway is a dual-degree program by way of engineering. Usually in these programs, three years are spent at one school focusing on non-engineering subjects, followed by two years at a different engineering-specific college, and often resulting in two degrees in five years. You will find several dual-degree or 3/2 engineering programs in this book, so let's pause here to discuss why you might consider engineering, even if you've never given much thought to it before.

These days, "engineer" describes a wide variety of professionals who earn impressive salaries in more than twenty-five specialties, including aerospace, chemical, civil, industrial, environmental, mechanical, and computer engineering. Once the virtually exclusive province of men wearing notched short-sleeve button-downs with plastic pocket protectors, these fields are increasingly popular with women as well, and there is no dress code. You *will*, however, be taking a healthy dose of math and science, and the requirements for engineering back gateways range from moderately difficult to very difficult. But there has never been a more opportune time to consider an engineering career, which may be expected to offer endless opportunity as new technologies continually emerge. Moreover, cooperative engineering programs allow you to become an engineer even as you study art, literature, and humanities. Many authorities on industry and education have pointed out that a growing roster of employers in technical fields are looking for qualified engineering graduates who also have a background in the broader liberal arts. This potentially makes the engineering back gateway much more than a "second chance" for students who could not enter their dream school via the front gate. A dual-degree or 3/2 engineering program may just make you the most prime of prime candidates for a great career.

Offered by Columbia's FU Foundation School of Engineering and Applied Science, the five-year program awards a B.A. degree from one of ninety participating liberal arts colleges and a B.S. degree from Columbia University. Students complete the requirements for the liberal arts degree, along with a pre-engineering course of study in three years at one of the partner colleges, then complete two years of engineering at Columbia University. The cooperating institutions are:

Adelphi University, Garden City, NY
Albion College, Albion, MI
Alfred University, Alfred, NY
Allegheny College, Meadville, PA
Arcadia University, Glenside, PA
Augustana College, Sioux Falls, SD
Austin College, Sherman, TX
Baldwin-Wallace College, Berea, OH
Bard College, Annandale-on-Hudson, NY
Bard College at Simon's Rock, Great Barrington, MA
Barnard College, New York, NY
Bates College, Lewiston, ME

Beloit College, Beloit, WI
Bethany College, Bethany, WV
Birmingham-Southern College, Birmingham, AL
Bowdoin College, Brunswick, ME
Brandeis University, Waltham, MA
Carleton College, Northfield, MN
Carroll College, Helena, MT
Centenary College of Louisiana, Shreveport, LA
Centre College, Danville, KY
Claremont McKenna College, Claremont, CA
Clark University, Worcester, MA
Colgate University, Hamilton, NY
College of Idaho, Caldwell, ID
College of the Holy Cross, Worcester, MA
College of William & Mary, Williamsburg, VA
Colorado College, Colorado Springs, CO
Columbia College, New York, NY
Davidson College, Davidson, NC
Denison University, Granville, OH
DePauw University, Greencastle, IN
Dillard University, New Orleans, LA
Doane College, Crete, NE
Drew University, Madison, NJ
Earlham College, Richmond, IN
Eckerd College, St. Petersburg, FL
Elon College, Elon, NC
Fairfield University, Fairfield, CT
Fordham University, Bronx, NY
Franklin & Marshall College, Lancaster, PA
Georgetown University, Washington, DC
Gettysburg College, Gettysburg, PA
Grinnell College, Grinnell, IA
Hamilton College, Clinton, NY

Hartwick College, Oneonta, NY
Hastings College, Hastings, NE
Hendrix College, Conway, AR
Hobart and William Smith Colleges, Geneva, NY
Hofstra University, Hempstead, NY
Illinois Wesleyan University, Bloomington, IL
Jacksonville University, Jacksonville, FL
Juniata College, Huntingdon, PA
Kansas Wesleyan University, Salina, KS
Knox College, Galeburg, IL
Lawrence University, Appleton, WI
Lewis & Clark College, Portland, OR
Loyola University Chicago, Chicago, IL
MacMurray College, Jacksonville, IL
Marietta College, Marietta, OH
Miami University, Oxford, OH
Middlebury College, Middlebury, VT
Millsaps College, Jackson, MS
Morehouse College, Atlanta, GA
Muhlenberg College, Allentown, PA
Nebraska Wesleyan University, Lincoln, NE
Notre Dame of Maryland University, Baltimore, MD
Oberlin College, Oberlin, OH
Occidental College, Los Angeles, CA
Pacific Lutheran University, Tacoma, WA
Pitzer College, Claremont, CA
Providence College, Providence, RI
Queens College, Flushing, NY
Randolph-Macon College, Ashland, VA
Reed College, Portland, OR
Rollins College, Winter Park, FL
St. John Fisher College, Rochester, NY
St. Lawrence University, Canton, NY

Sarah Lawrence College, Bronxville, NY

School of General Studies, Columbia University, New York, NY

Scripps College, Claremont, CA

Seattle Pacific University, Seattle, WA

State University of New York, Binghamton, NY

State University of New York, Fredonia, NY

State University of New York, Geneseo, NY

Sweet Briar College, Sweet Briar, VA

University of Puget Sound, Tacoma, WA

University of Richmond, Richmond, VA

University of the South, Sewanee, TN

University of the Virgin Islands, St. Thomas, VI

Ursinus College, Collegeville, PA

Wabash College, Crawfordsville, IN

Washington & Jefferson College, Washington, PA

Wesleyan University, Middletown, CT

Whitman College, Walla Walla, WA

Yeshiva University, New York, NY

Spelman College, Atlanta, GA

According to program officials, admission to Columbia is guaranteed if you meet the affiliated college's requirements, have been enrolled for two years, have maintained an overall grade point average of 3.0 or higher, and have successfully completed the science and math prerequisite courses listed in Columbia's Pre-Combined Plan Curriculum Guide.

*Alternative 3.* As promised, there is a third alternative to front-gate Columbia admission. However, it seems wrong to call it a "back gateway," and it has one very significant exclusion: men.

Located a few blocks from the Columbia campus, Barnard College is a women's institution, whose students, as the school's website explains, "have unrestricted access to Columbia University classes, professors, libraries, and events, while still maintaining their own campus and faculty, which are open to Columbia students."

Courses for some Barnard majors, including physics and East Asian language and cultures, are offered exclusively on the Columbia University campus. Conversely, Columbia's own theater, dance, and art history departments are housed at Barnard College. "While people might only imagine Barnard students running across the street to take classes at Columbia," the college website observes, "Columbia students are also found in Barnard classes depending on their major, personal interests, a particular professor, or interest in smaller class sizes."

The Columbia-Barnard partnership dates back more than a hundred years, during which the two institutions have shared a commitment that is "unique in American higher education and one that benefits students at both institutions." Barnard was founded in 1889 mainly through the efforts of Annie Nathan Meyer, an advocate of higher education for women, and was named after Columbia's tenth president (1864–1889), Frederick A. P. Barnard. He believed that women deserved an education comparable to that provided by Columbia and the other Ivy League schools, which were only open to men at the time. Although independently incorporated and financed, with its own administration and faculty, Barnard is also an official college of Columbia University. Students at each school can take courses at the other. Barnard graduates receive the diploma of Columbia University signed by the presidents of both institutions, but it is important to understand that Barnard is not subordinate or inferior to Columbia. In fact, the school is often hailed as one of the "Hidden Ivies."

Barnard certainly does not have to justify itself as a back gateway into Columbia. Although the acceptance rate for the Class of 2014 was 26.5 percent—slightly more than twice that of Columbia—it is still classified as "most selective" by *U.S. News & World Report*, which most recently ranked it the twenty-sixth best liberal arts college in the United States. The school's Committee on Admissions explains that it "selects young women of proven academic strength who exhibit the potential for further intellectual growth." The committee takes into consideration applicants' "high school records, recommendations and standardized test scores" as well as "the candidates' special abilities and interests."

## HOUSING AND TUITION

Tuition schedules vary for GS students, depending on whether they are enrolled full- or part-time. The latest cost of attendance (COA) figures are available on the GS website, but it is important to remember that work-study opportunities and financial aid packages are available.

As for housing, GS students may commute from home, find their own local housing, or apply to live in university apartment housing (UAH), which includes a variety of apartments and dormitory-style suites located within walking distance to campus. In some cases, UAH can even provide housing to couples and students with children; however, they warn that "demand exceeds supply" and so it "is not guaranteed for GS students." Even if UAH cannot accommodate you, you can still take advantage of Columbia's Off-Campus Housing Assistance Office (OCHA), which will help connect you with a suitable non-university-owned rental.

For more information, contact:

Columbia University
School of General Studies
408 Lewiston Hall MC4101
New York, NY 10027
(212) 854-2772
Website: www.gs.columbia.edu
Email: gs-admit@columbia.edu

Engineering Graduate Student Services Office
524 SW Mudd
500 W. 120th Street
New York, NY 10027
(212) 854-6438
Website: www.studentaffairs.columbia.edu
Email: seasgradmit@columbia.edu

The Jewish Theological Seminary
Albert A. List College of Jewish Studies
3080 Broadway
New York, NY 10027
(212) 678-8832
Website: www.jtsa.edu
Email: lcadmissions@jtsa.edu

Barnard College
3009 Broadway
New York, NY 10027
(212) 854-2014
Website: www.barnard.edu/admiss/
Email: admissions@barnard.edu

# 5

## Cornell University:
## "Any Person . . . Any Study"

> ### ▨ KEYBOX
>
> SCHOOL: Cornell University
>
> LOCATION: Ithaca, New York
>
> COLLEGE RANKING: 15
>
> GATE POSITION: Wide open
>
> SAT REQUIRED: No
>
> HOUSING: Limited
>
> MINIMUM AGE: 18
>
> APPLICATION CRITERIA: Moderate
>
> MEDIAN STARTING SALARY: $58,000
>
> COST COMPARED TO FRONT GATEWAY: Half

Ezra Cornell, the self-made telegraph mogul who cofounded Cornell University in 1865, declared, "I would found an institution where any person can find instruction in any study." This boldly democratic philosophy of education, now the university's official motto, marks Cornell as something of an Ivy League oxymoron: a very *exclusive* school with a very *inclusive* attitude.

Tied for fifteenth place among national universities in the 2013 *U.S. News & World Report* rankings, Cornell has often been described as the "easiest Ivy to get into," which, even if it were true, would remain a very relative judgment. For 2012, the admission rate was 18 percent—"easier" than Harvard's 6.3 percent, Columbia's 7 percent, and Penn's 12.4 percent. Yet, once admitted, some students feel that they've entered an academic pressure cooker. The 2008 *Fiske Guide to Colleges* describes the university's academic requirements as "challenging and demanding." In contrast, the school's setting is bucolic, by turns soothing and breathtaking. It is sited on three thousand scenic acres in upstate Ithaca, New York, and affords many panoramic hilltop views of Cayuga Lake. The average undergraduate enrollment is nearly fourteen thousand.

## FROM THE BEGINNING, A FOCUS ON TECH AND THE APPLIED SCIENCES

Ezra Cornell was the son of a potter and a first cousin (five times removed) of Benjamin Franklin. He started out life as an itinerant carpenter, but ended up working with telegraph inventor Samuel F. B. Morse to create what became the vast electrical communications network known as Western Union. With Andrew Dickson White, a historian (first president of the American Historical Association) and diplomat (U.S. ambassador to Germany and to Russia), Cornell founded the school in 1865 on what was then a radical theme of diversity, though one entirely suitable to a nation that had just fought a Civil War in large part over issues of equality and human rights. Although the first class enrolled in 1868 consisted of 412 young men, women were admitted beginning in 1870, making Cornell the first of the Ivy League to go coeducational. Virtually from the beginning, enrollment was open to all individuals, regardless of race or religion.

From the start, Cornell University emphasized science and technology. Swiss-born Louis Agassiz, perhaps the most famous American scientist of the mid nineteenth century, was among the very first faculty members. In 1883, Cornell became one of the world's first campuses to generate its own electricity to light its grounds. Although Cornell is a private university, it is also a land grant college, one of only two in the nation. All of the other land grant colleges are state schools.

As such, Cornell joined the ranks of academic institutions founded as part of a progressive nineteenth-century congressional mandate that ceded federal lands to support new colleges for the education of the "industrial classes." Since 1894, Cornell University has included state-funded statutory colleges and has carried out research and extension activities jointly funded by state and federal matching funds. Today, four of Cornell's seven undergraduate colleges operate with substantial assistance from New York State, including the College of Veterinary Medicine, the College of Agriculture and Life Sciences, the College of Human Ecology, and the College of Industrial and Labor Relations.

Cornell's Manhattan campus opened in 2013: Cornell NYC Tech, a grad school in partnership with Tehnion-Israel Institute of Technology. By 2037, the new Cornell Tech will be the home for two thousand students at a newly constructed campus on New York City's Roosevelt Island. When it opened in 2013, it was in temporary facilities at Google's New York offices.

## CORNELL'S BACK GATEWAY

Thanks to its land grant status, Cornell has long administered many extension programs and offers them in every New York State county. The university also has articulation agreements with twenty-one New York State community colleges that guarantee transfer admission to Cornell's College of Agriculture and Life Sciences (CALS) for students who meet specific academic requirements. They must:

1. Complete required courses for their intended CALS major with a B or better
2. Earn at least a 3.0 cumulative GPA overall

3. Complete the Cornell transfer application and meet all specified application deadlines
4. Submit an essay that successfully demonstrates their "solid interest and fit in the CALS major" for which they are applying
5. Commit to full-time study

If you meet these criteria and are in good academic and disciplinary standing, you are guaranteed admission to the following CALS major degree programs:

Agricultural Sciences
Agricultural Science Education
Animal Science
Applied Economics and Management (but only with concentrations in Agribusiness Management, Environmental Economics, or Food Industry Management)
Atmospheric Science
Biological Engineering
Biometry and Statistics
Communication
Development Sociology
Entomology
Environmental Engineering
Food Science
Information Science
International Agriculture and Rural Development
Natural Resources
Nutritional Sciences
Plant Sciences
Science of Earth Systems
Science of Natural and Environmental Systems
Viticulture and Enology

For the set of CALS majors listed below, transfer admission is *not* guaranteed, but you may apply as a "competitive transfer applicant." Your admission will be evaluated based on the appropriateness of your interests and fulfillment of other GPA, course, and profile requirements. These majors are:

Applied Economics and Management (Accounting, Applied Economics, Entrepreneurship, Finance, International Trade and Development, Marketing and Strategy)
Biological Sciences
Biology and Society
Landscape Architecture

Community colleges with guaranteed CALS transfer agreements include:

Alfred State College, Alfred, NY
Broome Community College, Binghamton, NY
Corning Community College, Corning, NY
Cortland Community College, Cortland, NY
Cumberland County College, Vineland, NJ
Farmingdale State College, East Farmingdale, NY
Finger Lakes Community College, Canandaigua, NY
Fulton-Montgomery Community College, Johnstown, NY
Jamestown Community College, Jamestown, NY
Jefferson Community College, Watertown, NY
LaGuardia Community College, Long Island City, Queens, NY
Monroe Community College, Brighton, NY
Morrisville State College, Morrisville, NY
Onondaga Community College, Syracuse, NY
Rockland Community College, Suffern, NY
Suffolk Community College, Selden, NY

SUNY Canton, Canton, NY
SUNY Cobleskill, Cobleskill, NY
SUNY Delhi, Delhi, NY
Thompkins Cortland Community College, Dryden, NY
Ulster Community College, Stone Ridge, NY

If you do not attend any of the schools listed above, or if you are not interested in any of the listed majors, or if you want to enroll in a Cornell college other than CALS, don't walk away yet. Cornell University encourages students who attend other community colleges or who want to pursue majors not offered at CALS to seek transfer to Cornell as "competitive transfer applicants." If the word "competitive" puts you off, be aware that Cornell is considered a very "transfer-friendly" school. During 2007–2008, for instance, 669 of 2,479 transfer applicants were offered admission. CALS, the *most* transfer-friendly of Cornell's seven colleges, accepted 297 of 577 transfer applicants, compared with 58 of 476 applicants to the College of Arts and Sciences, and 17 of 90 applicants to the School of Architecture. CALS enrolled about 250 transfer students in the fall semester, and 50 in the spring, which was nearly one-third of the enrolling class. The university reaches out with an annual informational "Transfer Day" and even offers rejected freshman applicants a guaranteed transfer acceptance one year later, provided they make good grades in the interim.

## HOUSING AND TUITION

The tuition schedules for Cornell's CALS program are available on the CALS website or by contacting admissions personnel directly. It is certain that you will pay less for a Cornell degree through the CALS program than through the university's traditional front gateway admission programs. Moreover, because of its land grant status, Cornell opens the door to New York State residents at downright bargain prices. For example, tuition for the CALS program in 2012–2013 was $27,273 for New York State residents versus $43,413 for nonresidents. In addition, because transfer to CALS is a 3/2 program, the school offers "prorated tuition," which allows students to pay separately for tuition at the transfer school and at CALS. Community college tuition is, of course, significantly lower than that at Cornell.

On-campus housing is not guaranteed for CALS transfer students. Nevertheless, it is worth taking a shot at securing a home on campus. School officials advise you to "contact the exchange office for up-to-date information."

In general, because 3/2 transfers are "upper-level" students, they are encouraged to live off-campus in the West Campus House System or in one of Cornell's eight cooperative houses (or "co-ops"). Log on to www.campuslife.cornell.edu/campuslife/housing/index.cfm for the latest information.

## How to Apply

You can apply to one of the seven colleges through Cornell's Undergraduate Admissions Office (address listed below) or online at www .commonapp.org/CommonApp/default.aspx. There is one important caveat: Admission standards vary significantly by school, but do bear in mind Cornell's transfer-friendly reputation and don't hesitate to try for the program of your dreams.

For more information, contact:

Undergraduate Admissions Office
Cornell University
410 Thurston Avenue

(607) 255-5241
Website: http://admissions.cornell.edu/

Agriculture and Life Sciences
177 Roberts Hall
(607) 255-2036
Website: www.cals.cornell.edu
Email: als_admissions@cornell.edu

Architecture, Art and Planning
B1 W. Sibley
(607) 255-4376
Website: www.aap.cornell.edu/admissions
Email: aap_admissions@cornell.edu

Arts and Sciences
172 Goldwin Smith
(607) 255-4833
Website: www.as.cornell.edu/admissions/index.cfm
Email: as_admissions@cornell.edu

Industrial and Labor Relations
216 Ives Hall
(607) 255-2222
Website: www.ilr.cornell.edu/admissions/

# 6

# A Tradition of Excellence: Yale University

> ### ■ KEYBOX
>
> SCHOOL: Yale University
>
> LOCATION: New Haven, Connecticut
>
> COLLEGE RANKING: 3
>
> GATE POSITION: Ajar
>
> SAT REQUIRED: No, but "highly recommended"
>
> HOUSING: None
>
> MINIMUM AGE: 18
>
> APPLICATION CRITERIA: Moderate
>
> MEDIAN STARTING SALARY: $56,000
>
> COST COMPARED TO FRONT GATEWAY: Half (Whitney only)

Like Harvard, *Yale* is a name that many desire intensely, and aspiring Yalies typically start their craving from a very early age. Matthew wasn't yet in his teens when he announced his intention to go to Yale University. He worked hard at school and built up an impressive GPA. By the time he was a junior, he vowed that nothing would stand in his way to New Haven.

Then he took the SAT. The results were disappointing. He took it two more times and managed to inch upward, but in fourth and fifth go-rounds he started to lose ground. One thing was certain. His scores were far below what the Yale Admissions Committee wanted to see, especially with acceptance rates in the single digits.

Matthew was stopped by a small set of numbers.

He decided to enroll in a small church-affiliated liberal arts college, and he did very well his freshman year. In his second semester, he became involved in a church-sponsored program to aid homeless families. He soon found that this work both absorbed and fulfilled him, and he left college at the end of his freshman year to devote himself to the homeless project full-time. After five years, however, his Yale dreams resurfaced. Soon, this was practically all he could think about. In the wake of his unexceptional SAT performance, Matthew had resigned himself to burying the dream. After all, numbers were numbers, and there was no appealing them.

True. There was no appealing the numbers, but, as he soon discovered, there *was* an alternative to them: a back gateway into Yale that gave you credit for achievement and for academic potential the SAT does not measure.

## EXCLUSIVITY AND POWER (AND A TOMB)

In its 2013 edition of *Best Colleges*, *U.S. News & World Report* ranked Yale University third overall among American universities. Although all of the Ivy League schools have a collective reputation for producing leaders in government, commerce, science, and the arts, the sense of power emanating from New Haven is especially strong. In part, this is due to the mysterious Skull and Bones secret society, which is headquartered on campus at 64 High Street in a windowless building affectionately dubbed the "Tomb." Just fifteen members of the junior class are "tapped" for membership each year, and, overwhelmingly, they are indeed members of a powerful elite that has included three generations of Bushes (Senator Prescott Bush and Presidents George H. W. and George W. Bush), Senator John Kerry, President William Howard

Taft, Walter Camp ("inventor" of American football), Henry L. Stimson (longtime U.S. secretary of war), Henry Luce (cofounder of the Time-Life publishing empire), H. J. Heinz II (ketchup heir), McGeorge Bundy (JFK administration insider and an architect of the Vietnam War), William F. Buckley Jr. (famed conservative and founder of the *National Review*), and David McCullough (Pulitzer Prize–winning historian and biographer).

Yale's aura of ultra-exclusivity and power is hardly confined to Skull and Bones. The university has produced seventeen Nobel laureates and twenty-four Pulitzer Prize winners. Inventors and innovators like Revolutionary War submarine pioneer David Bushnell, cotton gin genius Eli Whitney, neurosurgery innovator Harvey Williams Cushing, telegraph originator Samuel F. B. Morse, and child-rearing guru Dr. Benjamin Spock were all Yale graduates, as were business giants Hugh Auchincloss (Standard Oil), John F. Mars (of Mars candy fame), and Roberto Goizueta (late CEO of Coca-Cola). The reputation of power surrounding Yale is fully substantiated by the history Yale graduates have made and continue to make: five U.S. presidents, including four of the last six; forty-five cabinet members; and more than five hundred members of Congress.

Yale took a long time in its founding. As early as the 1640s, Connecticut clergymen discussed establishing an institution to bring the tradition of liberal education long cherished in Europe to the colonies. It was not until 1701, however, that the "Collegiate School" was chartered in Saybrook, Connecticut, to educate students for "Publick employment both in Church & Civil State." Fifteen years later, the school was moved to New Haven. In 1718 it was renamed Yale College to honor Welsh-American merchant Elihu Yale, who had donated 417 books, a portrait of King George I, and the proceeds of the sale of "nine bales of goods."

Founded to bring the Western European tradition of learning to America, Yale began attracting international students early in the nineteenth century. Today, international students make up nearly 9 percent of the undergraduate student body and 16 percent of the total student population. Yale began admitting women as graduate students in 1869, but not as undergraduates until 1969.

## A SYNTHESIS OF OLD AND NEW

Yale has long been known for combining innovation with tradition. Early in the 1930s, the school looked back to the example of such medieval English universities as Oxford and Cambridge to develop a residential undergraduate college system unique among American institutions. Yale undergrads are divided into twelve "colleges"—Berkeley, Branford, Calhoun, Davenport, Ezra Stiles, Jonathan Edwards, Morse, Pierson, Saybrook, Silliman, Timothy Dwight, and Trumbull—each containing about 450 students. In this way, the university offers something of a small college environment in the context of a major research university. The residential college idea is reflected in the physical structure of the campus, with each college housed in buildings surrounding its own courtyard. Every college is presided over by its own master and dean in addition to resident faculty members called fellows. Each college has its own dining hall, library, seminar rooms, and recreation lounges.

The Yale colleges are all located on the university's 310-acre campus, a collection of 260 buildings that represent a dazzling variety of architectural periods, styles, and distinguished architects. Located in otherwise gritty downtown New Haven, the campus has been praised as the "most beautiful urban campus in America."

Yale today enrolls some 11,593 students—including 5,275 undergraduates (more than Princeton, fewer than Harvard)—who come from all fifty states and 108 countries. They are taught by 3,619 faculty members, all of them leaders in their fields and most of them committed to teaching undergraduate as well as graduate courses.

The third-oldest institution of higher learning in the United States,

Yale enjoys a $19.4 billion endowment, second only to Harvard's. Yale's library holds 12.5 million volumes, also second only to Harvard's. With all that it has to offer, Yale attracts far more applicants than it accepts. For the Class of 2016, the university had a record-low 6.8 percent acceptance rate.

## YALE'S FIRST BACK GATEWAY

In 2012, 92.3 percent of those who applied to Yale were turned away at the front gate. Relatively few of them knew enough even to try this first back gateway, which you are about to discover.

It is called the Eli Whitney Students Program, named for the inventor of the cotton gin, who graduated with the Class of 1792. It is by no means a get-into-Yale-easy card. The website (http://admissions.yale.edu/eli-whitney#admissions) cautions that "Yale is only able to admit a small number of applicants" to the program each year, and that admission criteria are just as stringent for the program as for traditional, front-gateway undergraduate applicants. Nevertheless, the Eli Whitney Students Program provides a unique opportunity "to applicants whose work/life experience and community involvement promise to add unusual dimensions to undergraduate life in the classroom."

The admissions committee "looks especially for non-traditional students who have intellectual depth and curiosity, strong motivation, energy, and leadership. An applicant's interdisciplinary academic strength (especially in writing and quantitative reasoning) and achievement in career and community are also important factors." Although the minimum age for admission is eighteen and the only absolute educational prerequisite is a high school or GED diploma, the program is clearly geared toward somewhat older students, especially those who have already completed some college. "We strongly recommend," the admission website states, "that applicants submit records demonstrating recent excellent performance in demanding college courses." Moreover, applicants "must have taken at least a five-year break from [their] education." As university president Rick Levin puts it, the program seeks "students of exceptional promise and character, whose life circumstances have prevented them from completing a liberal arts degree in the traditional sequence."

If you are accepted into the Eli Whitney Students Program, you will enjoy access to all of Yale's undergraduate classes and facilities *except* for university housing or residential college housing. At the end of it all, you will be awarded a degree from Yale College of Yale University. That's *the* Yale.

## WHITNEY LIFE

Whitney program students must meet the same course requirements that apply to regular undergraduates. For a bachelor's degree, this means successfully completing a total of thirty-six term course credits. The Eli Whitney Students Program is tailored to the nontraditional student and therefore offers a flexible path to satisfying the standard requirements. You may attend Yale either full- or part-time, taking up to nine—but at least three—course credits each year. You don't need to earn all thirty-six credits at Yale. At least eighteen of your credits must come from Yale courses, but the university will accept as many as eighteen transfer credits earned at another college or university. Transfer credits, which must be from an accredited postsecondary institution, must have been earned for courses similar in content to those at Yale College. You must have earned grades of A or B in at least three-quarters of your non-Yale courses, and no lower than a C in the remainder. You have up to seven years to complete the degree.

As a Whitney program student, all majors are open to you. Like other Yale undergraduates, you will take eleven to fourteen courses in your major and also must meet other course distribution requirements, including taking at least two course credits in the humanities and arts, two in the sciences, and two in the social sciences. You will also need to fulfill standard undergraduate "skills requirements" by taking at least two course credits in quantitative reasoning, two course credits in writing, and courses in a foreign language. This latter requirement is flexible, depending on your level of accomplishment in foreign languages at the time of your enrollment.

## How to Apply

Application requires paying a $75 fee and submitting all materials by April 1. (Financial aid applications are due by May 1.) You will be required to:

- List all high schools, postsecondary institutions, and colleges and universities you have attended.
- Submit official transcripts.
- Furnish the dates and scores of SAT or ACT exams. (Although standardized tests are "not absolutely required," the university "strongly recommends" taking the SAT Reasoning Test [SAT I] or the ACT test; however, neither the SAT Subject Tests [SAT II] nor the Achievement Test are required or even recommended.)
- List all work experience.
- Submit three letters of recommendation, either from academic professors or employers and colleagues.
- Submit a personal statement of 300 to 600 words, which includes your reasons for applying to the Eli Whitney Students Program, and your personal and academic goals.

Complete application instructions and all necessary forms (including financial aid forms) are available online at http://admissions.yale.edu/eli-whitney-students-program-application-instructions-forms.

If, after reviewing your completed application, the admissions committee judges you to be among what it describes as the "strongest candidates," you will be asked to an interview. Although the interview is a mandatory requirement, you can arrange to conduct it by telephone or Skype if you are unable to travel to the Yale campus to do it in person.

## HOUSING AND TUITION

Students in the Eli Whitney Students Program may attend either full- or part-time, and tuition is determined according to the number of course credits you take. In the 2012–2013 academic year, the tuition was $4,700 per course credit. If this sounds expensive, keep in mind that the school awards financial aid based on financial need. You may apply for financial aid when you apply for admission.

Whitney program students are welcome to take part in a variety of on-campus events and activities and, if they attend full-time, may also participate in Yale's student health care program. They have access to all Yale facilities available to other undergraduates except for housing in the university's residences. This said, the university can assist you in your search for off-campus housing.

## YALE-NUS OPTION: A SECOND BACK GATEWAY

If study abroad is an option for you, then consider Singapore, location of Yale-NUS, which opened in August 2013. This back gateway involves living almost four years in the Republic of Singapore, where, fortu- nately for many, English is the primary language. Until 1963, it was part of the United Kingdom. Although most Yale-NUS students are from Singapore, others are admitted from India and China, as well as the rest of the world, including the Americas.

I'll jump right to what's important: It is hard to get into and pre- liminary acceptance rates are less than 10 percent. This Yale-NUS back gateway may only be marginally less difficult than Yale's front gateway, but nonetheless provides an additional way to get an Ivy League brand.

Your diploma will indeed have "Yale" on it, although it will be "issued by" the National University of Singapore (NUS). The magic words on that diploma read "Yale-NUS College," but if that is not good enough for you, read on for a third back gateway to a Yale degree. But for that one, first you will need to understand Yale-NUS.

Your Yale-NUS diploma will read either "Bachelor of Arts with Honours" or "Bachelor of Science with Honours" (that's "Honours" with the British spelling). You will have fourteen majors to choose from: anthropology, arts and humanities, economics, environmental studies, global affairs, history, life sciences, literature, mathematical and computational sciences, philosophy, philosophy-politics-economics, physical sciences, psychology, and urban studies.

So are graduates of Yale-NUS actual Yale alumni and allowed valuable membership in the Association of Yale Alumni (AYA)? The answer is yes, *kind of.* Yale-NUS grads are "international affiliates" in AYA, and have full access to the online AYA website and database. They can be part of some events and programs sponsored by AYA, but they cannot be voting members, officers, or delegates. Yale-NUS grads are not "Yale alumni," but rather "Association of Yale Alumni international affiliates."

Since Yale-NUS grads will be listed in that database with their contact information, they will have many of the advantages afforded by AYA, including alumni connections and job opportunities.

Yale-NUS students spend a portion of their four years as undergrads outside of Singapore. They live for a selected period of time at the Yale College campus in New Haven, Connecticut. They can attend the New Haven campus for a summer, a semester, or a full academic year. Additionally, some Yale-NUS courses in Singapore include the ability to teleconference with Yale classes in New Haven.

## HOUSING AND TUITION IN SINGAPORE

As each student at Yale in New Haven is assigned to a residential college, providing them an additional unique identity, the same happens at Yale-NUS. The Singapore campus has three residential colleges, each its own complete community housing 330 students.

All students live in suites, with "sky gardens" atop modern high-rise structures completed in 2013. Like the campus in New Haven, residential colleges have late-night eateries, as well as traditional Yale outdoor courtyards. The dorm fee is $3,530 per semester, and includes all meals, but for 2013 and 2014 this fee is reduced by 50 percent.

The residential colleges are the setting for dining, studying, recreation, and living, including the afternoon gatherings at "Rector's Teas." The residential colleges have facilities for athletics, performance, and dance, as well as classrooms and faculty offices for professors.

Per-semester tuition varies for Singapore citizens, Singapore permanent residents, and international students. There are two semesters per year, and the per-semester rate for international students in 2013 is $15,000. There is a $271-a-year miscellaneous fee. Also, there are different fees for international students graduating from Yale-NUS who agree to work in Singapore following graduation. Since the Yale-NUS College is new, and the tuition varies for different students, you can get updated details at www.yale-nus.edu.sg/index.php/apply/tuition -financial-aid-scholarship/tuition-and-fees.html.

## APPLYING TO YALE-NUS

Yale-NUS College is designed to accommodate one thousand students, with an acceptance of about 250 a year. The initial 2013 class had 150 students. You must apply online, using one of three options:

1. The Common Application and Yale-NUS Supplement: This option is for those not wishing to apply to Yale College in New Haven, Connecticut, but rather only to Yale-NUS in Singapore.
2. The Common Application and Yale College Supplement: The option to share your Yale College application with Yale-NUS is made available on the Yale College Supplement, and if you select this checkbox, materials submitted to Yale College also will be shared with Yale-NUS. This option is for those who wish to apply to both Yale College and to Yale-NUS.
3. The Yale-NUS Application: The option to apply only to Yale-NUS.

So you can either share your Yale College application with Yale-NUS, or you can fill out the separate Yale-NUS application. If you are applying only to Yale-NUS and not Yale College in New Haven, use the Yale-NUS supplement.

The Yale College Supplement is an add-on to the Common Application. According to the Supplement, if you select the checkbox to share the application with Yale-NUS, this does not affect any admission decision at Yale College in New Haven.

Also, since Yale-NUS is located outside the United States, sharing the application with Yale does not violate the single-choice rule of Early Action (early admissions), which only applies to U.S. colleges.

According to the Yale College Admissions Office, here are the eight characteristics that Yale-NUS College is looking for in a prospective student:

1. Strong record of academic achievement
2. Demonstrated leadership potential
3. Critical thinker capable of rigorous and insightful analysis
4. Skilled to communicate effectively and engage meaningfully with fellow students

5. Motivated to stretch their capacities and make the best use of the College's extraordinary resources, both academic and non-academic
6. Genuine appreciation for different perspectives and individuals with different backgrounds, interests, and ambitions
7. Consideration for others and an interest to serve broader society
8. Resilience, flexibility, and leadership skills to solve problems and function as high-performing change agents in a variety of demanding careers

## A THIRD BACK GATEWAY TO YALE: FIVE-YEAR CONCURRENT DEGREE PROGRAM

Now that you understand Yale-NUS College, you are ready for the third back gateway that can provide you with a Yale University degree. While at Yale-NUS, if you are an environmental studies major, you will be able to also earn a degree through the Yale University School of Forestry and Environmental Studies in New Haven.

Under this program, after five years, you will have the undergraduate degree from Yale-NUS plus a master's degree from one of Yale University's thirteen professional schools. In addition to any other time spent at the Yale campus in New Haven while an undergrad, students in the five-year program spend one semester in New Haven during their junior or senior year, plus a full fifth year there.

If admitted to the YFES 5th Year Concurrent Degree Program, the master of environmental science (M.E.Sc.) or master of environmental management (M.E.M.) degree will be awarded by Yale University following completion of the additional year of study at YFES.

The M.E.Sc. degree is designed for students interested in "conducting scientific research that contributes toward basic and applied knowledge. The course of study includes formalized training in the philosophy, ethics, and practice of science."

The M.E.M. degree is designed for students pursuing "careers such as environmental policy, analysis, stewardship, education, consulting, or management concerning natural resource sustainability. The program aims to provide students with a scientific understanding of ecological and social systems, which then can be applied in a policy or management context."

Like all of Yale's back gateways, this program accepts only a small number of applicants: two to five a year (but perhaps growing!). This five-year program was created because of Yale's interest in the cultural and ecological diversity of the southeast Asian region surrounding the Yale-NUS campus.

For more information, contact:

Eli Whitney Program
Office of Undergraduate Admissions
Eli Whitney & Non-Degree Students Programs
P.O. Box 208234
New Haven, CT 06520-8234
(203) 432-9316
Website: www.yale.edu
Email: eliwhitney.students@yale.edu

Yale-NUS
Online only at
Website: www.yale-nus.edu.sg or http://admissions.yale.edu/yale-nus
Email: admissions@yale-nus.edu.sg

Yale University YFES 5th Year Concurrent Degree Program
Website: www.yale-nus.edu.sg/index.php/learning/concurrent
-degree-with-yfes.html

# 7

## Climbing College Hill: Brown University

---

**KEYBOX**

SCHOOL: Brown University

LOCATION: Providence, Rhode Island

COLLEGE RANKING: 15

GATE POSITION: Ajar

SAT REQUIRED: Yes

HOUSING: Limited

MINIMUM AGE: 20—but with significant restrictions

APPLICATION CRITERIA: Moderate/High

MEDIAN STARTING SALARY: $52,300

COST OF BACK GATEWAY COMPARED TO FRONT: Same

---

Angela was thirty-four when she decided it was time to think about going to college. A Rhode Island resident, she started taking some adult education classes at a local community college, but was decidedly underwhelmed by the experience. It seemed to her little more than an extension of high school. On the verge of setting aside once and for all those nagging dreams of higher education, she stumbled upon an exciting program offered at Brown University. The Ivy League school draws thousands of overachieving students from across the nation annually and is so highly selective that she had never remotely thought of it for herself.

The back gateway Angela found is called the Resumed Undergraduate Education (RUE) program. Stepping through this portal, she started work on a degree in public policy. Today, armed with a Brown diploma, she is applying to graduate school.

## TRADITION WITH INNOVATION

Brown is a private university sprawled across a 140-acre campus on a verdant hillside overlooking Providence, the capital of Rhode Island. Founded in nearby Warren as the College of Rhode Island in 1764, it is the third-oldest institution of higher education in the New England area and the seventh-oldest in the United States. The college relocated to its current Providence location on College Hill in 1770 and, in 1804, was named after alumnus Nicholas Brown (Class of 1786), a prominent local merchant who gave the institution a gift of $5,000. Founded in the colony revered as a haven of religious tolerance, Brown was the first of the Ivy League schools to open its doors to students of all religions. Today, it continues to cherish a heritage of liberal openness and is a magnet for top-notch faculty and top-tier students.

In its 2013 edition of *Best Colleges*, *U.S. News & World Report* ranked Brown second in the country for "excellence in undergraduate teaching" and fifteenth overall among American institutions of higher learning. The *Princeton Review* placed Brown students on its list of "Happiest Students" in the 2007 edition of *The Best 366 Colleges*.

Brown has the oldest undergraduate engineering program in the Ivy League, established in 1847, and at one time the school boasted the world's only History of Mathematics Department. Brown has always combined respect for tradition with a commitment to innovation. The institution's first building in Providence, red-bricked University Hall, built in 1770, still stands and is still used. The campus boasts 235 buildings on the city's East Side, a neighborhood that boasts the largest remaining collection of colonial homes in the country.

In 1850, the university's fourth president, Francis Wayland, issued a revolutionary call for the introduction of greater freedom in the undergraduate curriculum. He believed each student should be able to "study what he chose, all that he chose, and nothing but what he chose." This concept was amplified in 1969, when a group of Brown students and faculty proposed the "New Curriculum," which emphasized the liberalism of the liberal arts by giving students the broadest possible latitude in directing their own education. Not only did the New Curriculum define undergraduate education at Brown for the next four decades, it became known nationally as the "Brown Curriculum" and has profoundly influenced liberal arts education throughout the United States.

Brown's insistence that students become the architects of their own education, developing their own liberal arts core while remaining open to the ideas and experiences of others, has produced a long and varied list of notable alumni, which includes the likes of public education pioneer Horace Mann (Class of 1819), Supreme Court chief justice Charles Evans Hughes (Class of 1881), philanthropist John D. Rockefeller Jr. (Class of 1897), humorist and Marx Brothers screenwriter S. J. Perelman (Class of 1925), legendary IBM CEO Thomas J. Watson Jr. (Class of 1937), media mogul Ted Turner (Class of 1960), former Apple Computer CEO John Sculley (Class of 1961), and Black Entertainment Television (BET) chairwoman and CEO Debra L. Lee (Class of 1976).

Brown is a wonderful place to learn, especially for those driven to take an active hand in designing their own curriculum. Although Brown takes pride in seeking diverse applicants from "all walks of life, backgrounds, interests, and cultural heritages" without regard to "quotas of any kind," the admission rate for 2012 was just 8.9 percent. As the *Princeton Review* puts it, "The cream of just about any crop applies to Brown," so that "gaining admission requires more than a superior academic profile from high school." Nine out of ten who come calling at Brown's front gateway can expect to be turned away.

## BROWN'S BACK GATEWAY

Fresh out of high school, you will, unfortunately, find the back gateway to Brown closed tight. The school's Resumed Undergraduate Education (RUE) program, which offers full access to all undergraduate programs, courses, and extracurricular activities, is open only to students who have been out of high school for at least six years but who have not yet completed a four-year bachelor's degree at another institution. If this happens to describe you, you are welcome to apply.

If you are accepted into RUE, you will pay the same tuition and follow the same schedules as other undergraduates, except that because RUE students typically have full-time jobs or family obligations, you will find it possible to secure permission to study part-time. Although most RUE students do not request on-campus housing, it is open to them, subject to availability.

From its inception, the RUE program has been an option only for what the university itself describes as "a small number of students." In recent years, admission has been getting even more selective as RUE has become more widely known. According to the *New York Times*, eighty to one hundred adults apply each year to the program, of whom only about ten are admitted. This means that your prospects of entering Brown via the back gateway are only marginally better than those for entering through the front. But they *are* marginally better.

At any given time, there are about thirty RUE students attending Brown. They are fully matriculated candidates and can elect full-time or part-time study. They are diverse in age, as well as geographic and ethnic origin, and they are equally divided by gender. Many receive financial aid and (as Brown puts it) an "impressive number" go on to graduate school.

## How to Apply

RUE applicants who have taken the SAT or ACT are required to submit their scores, but the university advises that applicants will not be disqualified if they lack standardized test scores. Brown makes it clear that factors beyond the traditional measurements are taken into account in evaluating an applicant for RUE. Indeed, because the backgrounds of older students often vary significantly from those of the traditional Brown applicant, a separate RUE Admissions Committee evaluates the credentials of these candidates.

The committee reviews a prospective student's special circumstances and life experience as well as transcripts from high school and college (wherever courses were taken for credit). As a RUE candidate, you may apply for September or January admission, and you must complete application files for either admission date by February 15. You will be asked to submit a personal statement; a $75 application fee; two or three letters of recommendation, preferably from college instructors, but also from anyone "who would be best able to write about your abilities and recent activities"; transcripts from all secondary schools and colleges attended; and SAT and ACT scores, if available. Based on a review of the applications, the RUE Admissions Committee selects a small number of candidates for personal interviews, which are conducted in March, usually by telephone. Decision letters are mailed in May for both September and January admission.

## TUITION AND HOUSING

Financial aid is available but is more limited than what is offered to students in traditional undergraduate programs, who are admitted on a need-blind basis. Tuition for the academic year 2011–2012, for a standard course load of eight to ten classes, was $41,328. Students attending part-time are charged on a per course basis.

As for housing, RUE students are welcome to "hang their hat" in the dorm rooms of Miller Hall, the graduate and medical student housing area. According to the school's website, "While priority is given to graduate and medical students for housing, on a first-come first-served basis, RUE students are welcome to apply and housing requests are usually approved."

For more information, contact:

The College Admission Office
Brown University
Box 1876
Providence, RI 02912
(401) 863-2378
Website: www.brown.edu/admission

RUE Program, Admission Office
Eric Hunter, Ph.D.
Assistant Director of Admission
(401) 863-7917
Email: eric_hunter@brown.edu

# 8

# A Dual-Degree Alternative from Dartmouth College

> ## ▣ KEYBOX
>
> **SCHOOL:** Dartmouth College
>
> **LOCATION:** Hanover, New Hampshire
>
> **COLLEGE RANKING:** 10
>
> **GATE POSITION:** Half-open
>
> **SAT REQUIRED:** Yes
>
> **HOUSING:** None
>
> **MINIMUM AGE:** 18
>
> **APPLICATION CRITERIA:** Moderate
>
> **MEDIAN STARTING SALARY:** $58,200
>
> **COST COMPARED TO FRONT GATEWAY:** Variable

During his senior year of high school, Steven abandoned his plans to backpack across Europe with his friends, deciding instead to pursue a degree in civil engineering. However, his decision was made long after the application deadline for his school of choice, Dartmouth College. The conventional thing to do would have been to enroll at another school, then try for a sophomore transfer. But Steven was never satisfied with convention. He dug into the literature on Dartmouth and surfaced with an important discovery. It was a back gateway that would allow him to finish not one degree, but two, in five years—and even save some money along the way.

## FOUNDED BY A YALIE

The Reverend Eleazar Wheelock was a Congregational minister from Connecticut (Yale Class of 1733), who took in a Mohegan Indian boy named Samson Occom as a student in 1743. This experiment in education was sufficiently successful to move Wheelock to found Moor's Charity School in Lebanon, Connecticut, primarily to teach Native Americans. When he decided to expand the school into a college, he selected remote Hanover, New Hampshire, as its site, secured the land as a gift from New Hampshire's royal governor, and, with young Occom's aid, raised funds. On December 13, 1769, King George III chartered the college "for the education and instruction of Youth of the Indian Tribes in this Land . . . and also of English Youth and any others." Wheelock named it after William Legge, the second earl of Dartmouth, who had enthusiastically supported his efforts.

The motto of this ninth college founded in colonial America, *"Vox clamantis in deserto,"* or "The voice of one crying in the wilderness," suited its preacher founder (the source is biblical, Isaiah 40:1–3) as well as its location on what was the far frontier of the New England colonies. Even today, Hanover is a quiet and out-of-the-way setting, a quaint town overlooking the scenic Connecticut River, which flows along New Hampshire's border with Vermont. Populated by not quite eleven thousand residents, it is the quintessential "college town," peopled by townies mostly employed by, affiliated with, or otherwise dependent on the school, and dotted by quaint shops and restaurants that cater almost exclusively to Dartmouth students.

If Hanover appeals to folks who neither crave nor desire big-city lights, Dartmouth is ideal for students who want the advantages of a major Ivy League university *and* the intimacy of a private country college. Dartmouth enrolls only about 4,250 undergraduate and nearly 1,900 graduate students. The outstanding undergraduate program features small class sizes and a highly diverse faculty. In addition, the school offers nineteen graduate programs, including the renowned Dartmouth Medical School; the nation's first professional engineering school, the Thayer School of Engineering; and the first graduate school of management in the world, the Tuck School of Business, which was established in 1900.

Ranked tenth among national universities in *U.S. News & World Report*'s *Best Colleges 2013*, Dartmouth College attracts students from across the United States and around the world. It should therefore come as no surprise that admission is highly competitive. For the Class of 2016, more than 23,000 students applied. Of these, 10.1 percent were accepted.

If the odds are almost nine to one against your getting through Dartmouth's front gateway, the payoff for those who are admitted is high—not only in the quality of the educational experience, but in cash. According to the *Wall Street Journal*, Dartmouth graduates will earn a higher median salary ten years after graduation than alumni of any other American university surveyed.

## DARTMOUTH'S BACK GATEWAY

The good news is that Dartmouth does offer a back gateway. The bad news is that it is only for students who seek a degree in engineering. This said, bear in mind that engineering as taught at Dartmouth is unlike engineering taught anywhere else.

The distinguished Thayer School of Engineering was founded in 1867 by Dartmouth alumnus Brigadier General Sylvanus Thayer (Class of 1807), a U.S. Army engineer who served from 1817 to 1833 as superintendent of West Point. Thayer's impact on the United States Military Academy was so profound that he is often referred to as the "father of

West Point," and it was under his leadership that the academy's curriculum became heavily devoted to engineering. In 1867, Thayer donated what was at the time a staggering sum of $30,000 to create the first civilian professional school of engineering in the nation.

If you want to be an engineer, looking into the Thayer back gateway is an obvious move, but even if you've never seriously thought about pursuing an engineering degree, the program is worth considering. General Thayer endowed the school at his alma mater precisely because he believed in the idea of teaching engineering in the context of a liberal arts education as a means of preparing young people to more creatively address real-world problems and opportunities. A radical notion in the mid nineteenth century, linking engineering with the liberal arts is today the cutting-edge direction a number of engineering programs are beginning to take.

At Dartmouth, engineering undergraduates are not narrowly focused on numbers and technologies, but are thoroughly grounded in the liberal arts and rooted in the humanities. Major in engineering sciences, and you are a student in the Dartmouth bachelor of arts program, not the bachelor of sciences program. Many Thayer School undergraduates integrate their study of engineering with work in other sciences or even with studio art.

As Thayer engineering students develop professional skills, they are also required to take a range of courses in a variety of fields and disciplines. According to Thayer School leaders, "When expertise from across the engineering disciplines converges, the opportunities for groundbreaking innovation increase exponentially." This not only results in a creative academic philosophy that encourages students to share ideas, challenges, and solutions in an atmosphere of teamwork and convergence, it means that the engineering track also becomes an avenue to a broadly liberal education. Thus, even if you don't intend to pursue a career as an engineer, engineering can be your portal to a Dartmouth degree, and a more creative and remunerative working life.

As the Thayer website puts it, the School of Engineering "offers an energetic, hands-on learning community that develops passionate innovators who possess the intellectual and personal capacity to advance the world—and have fun doing it!" Its academic mission is rooted in both history and culture, even as it aims at "improving the present" and "shaping the future."

Majors within the Thayer School include engineering sciences, biomedical engineering, modified engineering sciences, and engineering physics, with minors available in materials science and engineering sciences.

## THE DUAL-DEGREE PROGRAM

Like students in Dartmouth's other schools, most Thayer students enter through the front gateway. But if you cannot (or choose not to) access the Thayer School in this way, you can apply to the Dual-Degree Program, which is specially designed for engineering students who want to study at Dartmouth.

It works like this.

You attend a participating "home college" for a total of three years, spending either your junior or senior year at Dartmouth, after which you receive a bachelor's degree from your home college. With this degree in hand, you return to Dartmouth to complete a fifth year of engineering studies in Thayer's professionally accredited bachelor of engineering program, from which you graduate with a Dartmouth B.E. degree. Thus, at the end of your undergraduate career, you hold two degrees: a non-Dartmouth B.A. and a Dartmouth B.E.

You may divide your home college/Dartmouth attendance in one of two ways:

Option I: The "2-1-1-1 Option"
Freshman and sophomore years: home college
Junior year: Dartmouth

Senior year: home college
Bachelor of engineering year: Dartmouth

### Option II: The "3/2 Option"
Freshman, sophomore, and junior years: home college
Senior year followed by the bachelor of engineering year: Dartmouth

## Participating "Home Colleges"

As of spring 2010, students from the following schools have participated in the dual-degree engineering program:

Bard College, Annandale-on-Hudson, NY
Bard College at Simon's Rock, Great Barrington, MA
Bates College, Lewiston, ME
Bowdoin College, Brunswick, ME
Carleton College, Northfield, MN
Colby College, Waterville, ME
College of the Holy Cross, Worcester, MA
Grinnell College, Grinnell, IA
Hamilton College, Clinton, NY
Hobart and William Smith Colleges, Geneva, NY
Middlebury College, Middlebury, VT
Morehouse College, Atlanta, GA
Mount Holyoke College, South Hadley, MA
Reed College, Portland, OR
Skidmore College, Saratoga Springs, NY
Smith College, Northampton, MA
Spelman College, Atlanta, GA
St. Lawrence University, Canton, NY
Vassar College, Poughkeepsie, NY
Wheaton College, Norton, MA

Even if your current or intended "home college" is not listed, Thayer officials invite you to pick up the phone and call them at (603) 646-3677. "We'll be happy," they say, "to talk with you about the possibility of joining the program."

## How to Apply

Understand that the Dual-Degree Program is demanding. To prepare for the program, you must take, *at your home college*, the core courses that all undergraduate engineering sciences majors take *at Dartmouth*. This means, at minimum:

- Calculus (through vector-valued functions, typically three courses)
- Physics (two courses through mechanics and electromagnetism)
- General chemistry (one course)
- Introduction to computer science and programming

The Dual-Degree Program accepts all Advanced Placement or International Baccalaureate credits awarded by the home college.

In addition to this preparatory core, the Thayer faculty recommends courses beyond the minimum, including courses in your science major or courses that support your specific engineering interest. The stronger your preparatory course work, the stronger your application and, therefore, the better your chances of gaining admission to what is a highly selective program.

Before applying, you are encouraged to consult with your home college dean or academic advisor during your first year. In most cases, you must receive approval from your home college to enter the program. After receiving approval, you may obtain an application form from the dual-degree advisor at your home college. Alternatively, you can request the form by contacting the Thayer School of Engineering at (603) 646-3677 or by emailing ugengg@dartmouth.edu. Or you can simply download the PDF application form from http://engineering.dartmouth.edu/

admissions/undergraduate/dual. Complete the form and return it as soon as your fall semester grades are available—but no later than February 1 of your sophomore year (for the Option I, 2-1-1-1 schedule) or junior year (for the Option II, 3/2 schedule)—to:

Dual Degree Program
Attn: Jenna Wheeler
Thayer School of Engineering, Dartmouth
8000 Cummings Hall
Hanover, NH 03755-8000

The form requires that you also submit:

- A personal statement of your reasons for applying to the program
- Official transcripts for each school you have attended
- A letter of recommendation from an academic advisor

In most cases, you will receive your admission decision by March 18. Occasionally, the admissions committee requests midterm grades for the spring semester, which does delay the decision. Admissions officials comment that, in recent years, they have received "many more applications than places in the program." For this reason, you may find yourself put on a waiting list "for reconsideration if space becomes available."

## WHAT TO EXPECT

As the comprehensive nature of the preparation required for the program suggests, engineering at Dartmouth is demanding. So it is a good idea to know up front what to expect.

During your first year *at Dartmouth*, you will take six undergraduate engineering sciences courses and two or three non-engineering courses, typically in the humanities or social sciences.

At your *home college*, you will need to satisfy B.E. requirements by taking at least nine courses in mathematics and natural science. These include prerequisites in calculus, physics, and chemistry in addition to upper-level courses. For science majors, the upper-level requirements are satisfied by the major courses. Nonscience majors must make certain to take upper-level courses in math and science that support their engineering interests.

The B.E. also requires a year of humanities (foreign language courses may be counted) and social sciences course work.

During your second year *at Dartmouth*, in the *Thayer School of Engineering*, you will complete the requirements for the B.E. degree. These consist of nine courses intended to develop proficiency in your chosen engineering field and to fulfill the other requirements for the degree. In sum, the B.E. degree requires a total of 24.5 courses, including at least nine in mathematics and natural science (counting the prerequisites) and at least 13.5 in engineering sciences (the 0.5 credit is provided by the computer science prerequisite).

You can get further details at http://engineering.dartmouth.edu/undergraduate/be/requirements.html.

## TUITION AND HOUSING

Naturally, the total cost of tuition depends on what home college you attend before transferring to Dartmouth. Assuming tuition costs less at your home college than at pricey Dartmouth, you will save money on your Ivy League education. Once you arrive at Hanover, however, you'll be writing checks to Dartmouth University.

It is not a cheap place. For 2012–2013, annual tuition and fees at Dartmouth were $45,042. Room and board added another $12,954. Financial aid is available to full-time students in the B.E. program, in the form of partial-tuition scholarships, hourly employment (as teaching assistants and in other capacities), fellowships, and loans. You can get more information and apply for aid at http://engineering.dartmouth .edu/admissions/financial-aid.html. For information and an application form for the Mazilu Engineering Research Fellowship, go to http:// engineering.dartmouth.edu/undergraduate/ab/mazilu.html.

First-year dual-degree students are eligible for Dartmouth undergraduate housing. Dormitories offer single and double rooms, quads, suite-style living, and three- and four-bedroom apartments. Each dormitory has its own style and character; some are modern in design, while others are of traditional brick-and-ivy Georgian architecture.

Second-year dual-degree students are *not* eligible for on-campus housing. Dartmouth does, however, offer information about the local rental market through the Dartmouth Real Estate Office, which you can visit in person or by email at engs@Dartmouth.edu.

For more information, contact:

Dartmouth College
6016 McNutt Hall
Hanover, NH 03755
(603) 646-2875
Website: www.dartmouth.edu
Email: admissions.office@dartmouth.edu

Dual-Degree Program
Thayer School of Engineering
Dartmouth College
8000 Cummings Hall
Hanover, NH 03755-8000
1-888-THAYER6 or (603) 646-3677

# 9

# Ivy on the Thames:
# Getting into Oxford

---

**▥ KEYBOX**

SCHOOL: University of Oxford

LOCATION: Oxford, England

WORLD COLLEGE RANKING: 5

GATE POSITION: Wide open

SAT REQUIRED: No

HOUSING: Yes

MINIMUM AGE: <18

APPLICATION CRITERIA: Moderate/High

MEDIAN STARTING SALARY: $50,000

COST COMPARED TO FRONT GATEWAY: Half

---

Oxford, more formally the University of Oxford, is the oldest university in the English-speaking world and is universally considered one of the most prestigious educational institutions anywhere. It was rated for 2011 by the UK's *Guardian* as that nation's number one university, and by *U.S. News & World Report*'s *Best Colleges 2013* as number five worldwide.

Oxford traces its history to at least 1096, although the precise date when teaching began at this Thames River village is subject to speculation and dispute. What we do know for certain is that the school received a needed medieval boost in 1167, when King Henry II banned English students from attending the then new University of Paris. This decree put Oxford on the academic map.

The University of Oxford alumni and former faculty include twenty-five British prime ministers, at least as many principal leaders of other nations, forty-seven Nobel laureates, a dozen saints, a half-dozen kings, and a score of archbishops of Canterbury, not to mention nine Olympic medalists. Even chosen at random, any list of notable "Oxonians" is bound to be both impressive and varied—for instance, Sir Walter Raleigh, Sir Thomas More, Roger Bacon, Lewis Carroll, Indira Gandhi, Hugh Grant, Rupert Murdoch, Tony Blair, King Abdullah of Jordan, and Rhodes Scholar Bill Clinton. In 2010, 107 Oxonians were members of the House of Commons and more than 140 sat in the House of Lords. Five members of the U.S. House of Representatives and four U.S. senators also attended Oxford.

## THE OXFORD MYSTIQUE

No other university in the world, not even Harvard or Yale, exercises over the academic imagination quite the same power as Oxford. It starts with the university's location in the town of Oxford, fifty-five miles northeast of London, on the River Thames. Called the "City of Dreaming Spires," for the iconic gothic architecture of the university buildings that dominate its skyline, Oxford is steeped in history and suffused with tradition.

If the setting of the university is exactly what you'd expect it to be—quietly busy yet contemplatively timeless—so the predominant teaching method is rooted deep in the institution's history. Most teaching consists of weekly essay-based tutorials conducted in the university's autonomous, independently governed colleges and halls. The tutorials are supplemented and supported by large lectures, and laboratory classes presented by faculty. Thus, an Oxford education is a combination of intimate tutorial and relatively large-scale lecture.

The University of Oxford actually consists of thirty-eight colleges and six Permanent Private Halls (PPHs), the latter of religious foundation. All degree candidates must belong either to one of the colleges or PPHs. The colleges function as the student's residence as well as the site of those tutorials that are at the heart of the Oxford teaching method. Like Yale in the United States—which uses the Oxford residential system as a model—students benefit from college-scale intimacy in the context of a vast university with world-class research and lecture facilities. Although candidates for admission to Oxford may name their preferred colleges, departmental officers often reallocate new students to ensure a reasonably equitable distribution among the colleges.

It is the individual Oxford college that creates much of the institution's characteristic environment. Each college has its own dining hall, chapel, library, and, in most cases, bar. Each college has commons rooms as well as dormitory accommodations for two to four hundred undergraduates. Thus, each college is in itself a small academic and social community.

## EXCELLENCE

The collegial climate created by Oxford's traditions, setting, and college system is essential to the educational experience there; however, it is the school's sheer academic excellence and advanced research facilities that draw students from 139 countries. Likewise, the faculty is also international, with nearly a third of the teaching and research staff coming from outside the UK. A select fraction of the international postgraduate student body study at Oxford on highly coveted Rhodes Scholarships.

Access to Oxford's socio-intellectual cachet and academic excellence is, of course, highly selective. It has always been so, but during the past thirty years, the number of undergraduate applications has more than doubled. Oxford invites about *80 percent* of the applicants for personal interviews. These are conducted around the world, including in the United States, source of the largest number of Oxford's international students—1,413 in 2008. University recruiters annually tour America; in 2010 they visited nine cities.

Admission standards for regular U.S. applicants are rigorous. Minimum standard requirements include the SAT Reasoning Test with a score of at least 700 in Critical Reading and Mathematics and preferably 700 or more in Writing; or an ACT with a score of at least 32 out of 36. In addition, applicants must have achieved a 5 in three or more Advanced Placement Tests in appropriate subjects or a 700 or higher in three appropriate SAT Subject Tests. Admissions officials caution that "competition for places is very strong and even excellent qualifications will not guarantee you a place. If you are not in a position to make a competitive application, you may wish to undertake further study before applying."

Overall, the university receives an average of four applications for each available place. This means that about a quarter of those who apply to Oxford are accepted; however, only about one in ten applicants from outside of the UK gain admission. This puts Oxford on par with most U.S. Ivy League schools in terms of extreme selectivity.

## OXFORD'S BACK GATEWAY

Like most of the American Ivies, Oxford does have a back gateway. It passes through the university's Department for Continuing Education, which annually offers courses to some fifteen thousand students on a part-time basis. For all its airs of exclusivity, Oxford was a nineteenth-century pioneer of the university extension movement which aimed to "extend" the benefits of a university education to the widest possible public. Today, the university offers more than six hundred short and part-time courses and has the fourth largest continuing education program in the United Kingdom. Included are evening and weekend classes, residential and summer schools, and online courses. Many of the courses carry undergraduate or graduate-level qualifications, though only courses of study in modern history or English literature and language lead to admission to an Oxford baccalaureate degree program.

The Department for Continuing Education offers an alternative path to a traditional Oxford diploma by enrolling students in the foundation certificate program, which is the equivalent of one year of regular full-time Oxford study taken part-time over two years. Earning the foundation certificate gives you a leg up to enrollment in a traditional, full-time program at one of the university's thirty-eight colleges. Acceptance for full-time study is by no means guaranteed, but is both competitive and at the discretion of the particular college. Nevertheless, what the university calls a "significant proportion" of students in the popular English literature program regularly move into full-time study at Oxford, while others choose to continue their education at other prestigious UK universities. Over half of the students who complete the modern history foundation certificate transfer to full-time Oxford colleges or other universities.

## THE FOUNDATION CERTIFICATE VERSUS OTHER "UNDERGRADUATE AWARDS"

Before we go on, it is important to understand that the Department for Continuing Education offers courses in a wide variety of fields; however, the department awards foundation certificates—the credential that will give you a probable one-in-two chance of gaining admission to regular full-time study at Oxford—only in modern history and English literature and language. There are other "undergraduate awards" available in other areas, such as archaeology and history of art, but these do not constitute a back gateway leading to a bachelor's degree at the University of Oxford.

## How to Apply

There are no age or academic requirements for admission to either the history or the English program, but you *are* expected to demonstrate "strong motivation." Along with your application you must submit a persuasive written statement of your reasons for wanting to enroll, along with a recommendation from a qualified reference.

Successful candidates for the English literature and language program should be "mature individuals who can show, both in their application and at interview, strong motivation and a prior interest in literature," according to the school's website.

For the modern history program, formal qualifications are "not essential," and students typically come from a "variety of backgrounds." The Continuing Education website advises that "if you have little or no recent experience of study or examinations, you should not be deterred from applying for a place on the course." While this is certainly a cordial invitation to apply, you should know that applicants are expected to demonstrate in their applications as well as their personal interviews a strong motivation to undertake the program and a prior interest in the study of history. And although there is no absolute qualifications requirement, your previous academic background will be taken into account in admission decisions.

Whether you apply to the history or the English program, your application must include basic biographical and educational information along with a three- to four-hundred-word statement of why you wish to enroll. You must also submit a "satisfactory reference" from someone qualified to assess your academic ability and attest to your motivation, commitment, and potential. You will be instructed to send your designated reference a form that asks whether you have "the necessary commitment and interest to pursue an intensive part-time course." Your reference will return the form to you in a sealed, signed envelope, which you will then send to Oxford, unopened, along with your application and statement.

### English Literature and Language

The English literature and language program includes six two-hour evening classes, in addition to a six-day summer school between the first and second years, and six daytime sessions over the two years of the program. In addition, instruction includes two one-hour tutorial sessions per term. You will take a written examination at the end of each year.

The program covers authors that include Shakespeare, Dickens, Hardy, Conrad, Yeats, and Wolfe, among others. The first year covers a range of topics, including Victorian literature and Renaissance poetry, while summer school is devoted exclusively to William Shakespeare. The second year includes modern critical theory, modernist literature, and Renaissance drama.

### Modern History

The modern history program consists of thirty two-hour weekly evening seminars and a nonresidential study week at the start of the second year. You will be required to write thirteen essays of 1,200 to 2,000 words each and one longer essay of 3,000 to 4,000 words. A written examination is given at the end of each year.

Course work covers British history during the periods of 1485–1603 and 1900–1979, European history from 1815 to 1914, and your choice of either the English nobility from 1560 to 1640 or the Spanish Civil War.

### Creative Writing

Another offering you should know about is the Department for Continuing Education's two-year, part-time course in creative writing. Unlike the English literature and language and modern history courses of study, the creative writing program is not the equivalent of a regular

Oxford freshman year, but culminates in the award of a master of studies (M.St.) degree. Oxford's only diploma in creative writing, the M.St. is technically a postgraduate degree but does not *absolutely* require applicants to have completed a bachelor's degree or other undergraduate study (collectively called a "first degree" in the UK). Indeed, the creative writing M.St. program has no rigid admission requirements at all, but does seek students with a "proven record of commitment to their craft" who exhibit an "open-minded, questioning approach to both reading and writing." You can find an application form and a *somewhat* more detailed discussion of recommended prerequisites at http://award bearing.conted.ox.ac.uk/creative_writing/howtoapply.php.

The first year of the program concentrates equally on prose fiction, poetry, and drama, while the second year offers students an opportunity to specialize in the genre of their choice, including the novel, short fiction, radio drama, television drama, screenwriting, stage drama, and poetry. Study is part-time and consists of a combination of five "residences" and two "guided retreats" at Oxford over two years, as well as study completed off campus. In addition, one "placement" gives students one to two weeks of "real world" experience in a literary agency, a publishing house, a literary periodical, a theater company, a screen production company, or other organization relevant to the student's specialized interest. Although much of the work is off campus, all M.St. students are "matriculated members of the University and one of its colleges." In other words, if you are accepted into the program, you *are* an Oxford University student.

The M.St. is not precisely the equivalent of a U.S. master's degree such as an M.A.; however, many universities in the UK as well as the United States recognize the degree as the basis for application to a Ph.D. or other graduate programs. As an Oxford degree, it is certain to have high value with employers everywhere, especially in publishing and related industries.

## TUITION AND HOUSING

Tuition rates and other fees can be somewhat complicated, depending on the course schedule you choose. It is best to deal with these issues when you complete your application package. The bottom line, however, is that the cost of the two-year foundation certificate program is generally about half that of the first year of Oxford for regular foreign undergraduates. As for housing, the university offers residential accommodations for full-time students, as well as housing for occasional overnight stays for part-time students. Full on-campus accommodations *are* provided for the residential portions of the M.St. program in creative writing.

For more information, contact:

Department for Continuing Education
University of Oxford
Rewley House
1 Wellington Square
Oxford OX1 2JA
United Kingdom
+44 (0)1865 270360
Website: www.ox.ac.uk
Email: enquiries@conted.ox.ac.uk

For the creative writing program, log on to http://awardbearing.conted .ox.ac.uk/creative_writing/mstcw.php.

# 10

## School of Kings:
## The University of Cambridge

---

**KEYBOX**

SCHOOL: University of Cambridge

LOCATION: Cambridge, England

WORLD COLLEGE RANKING: 1

GATE POSITION: Wide open

SAT REQUIRED: No

HOUSING: Yes

MINIMUM AGE: <18

APPLICATION CRITERIA: Moderate/High

MEDIAN STARTING SALARY: $50,000

COST COMPARED TO FRONT GATEWAY: Same

---

The second oldest university in the UK, Cambridge was founded in 1209 after a group of Oxford scholars, having fallen into a dispute with local townsfolk, decamped and resettled at Cambridge. Ancient though it is, Cambridge has long been known as a center for the most advanced and even epoch-making scientific study—its rival Oxford is better known for excellence in the humanities. It claims among its faculty and alumni more Nobel prizes than any other institution in the world: some eighty-two in all. Cambridge alumni have been responsible for breakthroughs in fundamental scientific knowledge and include

Francis Bacon, the late sixteenth- and early seventeenth-century formulator of the scientific method; Sir Isaac Newton, inventor of calculus and promulgator of the laws of physics; atom splitter Ernest Rutherford; evolutionary theorist Charles Darwin; Alan Turing, founder of modern computer science; and Francis Crick and James D. Watson, the duo who discovered the structure of DNA.

*U.S. News & World Report*'s *Best Colleges 2013* ranked Cambridge number one among the world's universities, as had QS World University Rankings in 2011. The university's famed publishing arm, Cambridge University Press, is not only the world's biggest and most prolific academic press, but also the oldest printer and publisher in the world. Today, the university is the UK's largest, with an enrollment of more than eighteen thousand, and it enjoys one of the world's richest academic endowments, at more than eight billion U.S. dollars.

## THE SILICON VALLEY OF THE UK

The city of Cambridge, seat of the university, is situated fifty miles northeast of London and is dominated by the gothic spires of the school's sixteenth-century King's Chapel. The stately antiquity of both the town and its university belies the fact that they are the core of the "Cambridge Cluster," also known as "Silicon Fen," a concentration of high-tech research and manufacturing facilities.

Even as Cambridge has long dominated the most advanced British science and technology, the university has also enjoyed the traditional patronage and favor of the British royal family. King Edward VII, King George VI, Prince Henry of Gloucester, and Prince William of Gloucester and Edinburgh were all students at Cambridge. Prince Charles, the present-day duke of Wales, is likewise a graduate, and his father, Prince Philip, the duke of Edinburgh, holds the ceremonial office of chancellor of the university. Other notable alumni include Oliver Cromwell, Lord Byron, Jawaharlal Nehru, Samuel Taylor Coleridge, John Maynard

Keynes, Vladimir Nabokov, Sylvia Plath, Bertrand Russell, Tennyson, the influential feminist theorist Germaine Greer, and John Cleese of Monty Python fame. Picturesque Cambridge has been the setting for numerous fictional works, ranging from Charles Dickens's *A Tale of Two Cities* and Jane Austen's *Pride and Prejudice* to the 1981 film *Chariots of Fire* and the final episode of television's *Star Trek: The Next Generation*.

As with Oxford, admission to Cambridge is highly selective, and the regular application process is extremely rigorous. For the 2011 academic year, Cambridge received 15,344 applications and accepted 3,879 of them—17 percent overall. Of those who applied from *outside* the UK, the university accepted fewer than 10 percent.

It is well known that only those with the very highest grades need apply to Cambridge. But great grades and monster test scores alone are not enough to gain admission. Most applicants are also interviewed face-to-face, some of them two or three times. Applicants from the United States are expected to have achieved what the school's recruiters call a "high pass" from high school grades and SAT tests, plus scores of 5 on at least two of three required advanced placement (AP) tests. Unlike Oxford, Cambridge does not conduct international recruiting tours, so U.S. and other overseas candidates for front gateway admission must come to the UK to answer any interview requests.

## CAMBRIDGE'S BACK GATEWAY

Cambridge's acceptance of about one-in-ten foreigners who apply makes the school's selectivity almost exactly equivalent to most U.S. Ivy League institutions. Moreover, the application process and the admissions requirements can be daunting and even expensive, especially for students from outside of the UK.

The back gateway offers an alternative. As with Oxford, Cambridge's back gateway runs through a continuing education program. The Cambridge version is called the Institute of Continuing Education

(ICE), and it has been serving part-time and adult students since the 1860s. Although geared primarily toward "mature"—especially working—students, ICE proclaims itself open to all "whether aged 18 . . . or 88." It is based at Madingley Hall, a stately sixteenth-century country manor located four miles west of Cambridge proper. The entire home was rented by Queen Victoria for the Prince of Wales—who became King Edward VII—when he was a Cambridge student.

You need to know up front that ICE is not a simple alternative pathway to a Cambridge undergraduate degree. Instead, study at ICE offers a variety of "qualifications" that represent varying levels of academic credit in the UK's Credit Accumulation and Transfer Scheme (CATS). Many of the qualifications are useful academic credentials in themselves, and the CATS credits associated with them can often be transferred to other Cambridge degree programs as well as to programs in other UK universities. Acceptance of CATS credits outside of the UK, including the United States, is widespread but neither guaranteed nor uniform in application. There is no straightforward, universally accepted set of correspondences between the Cambridge ICE program qualifications and U.S. degree program credits, transfer credits, and prerequisites.

The highest-level postgraduate diploma available through ICE are the two-year, part-time master of studies (M.St.) graduate degree, which is currently offered in twelve areas:

Advanced subject teaching
Applied criminology and police management
Applied criminology, penology and management
Building history
Construction engineering
Creative writing
Historic environment
Interdisciplinary design for the built environment

International relations
Local and regional history
Study of Jewish-Christian relations
Sustainability leadership

ICE periodically changes its offerings, adding some and discontinuing others.

The M.St. programs are *graduate-level* courses of study that culminate in a *graduate-level* diploma, which may be recognized by some U.S. universities and employers as the equivalent of standard U.S. master's degrees; in some cases, an M.St. may serve as the basis for further graduate study up to and including the Ph.D., whether at Cambridge or elsewhere.

Although most of the undergraduate courses at ICE are what admissions officials call "open-access" that do not require "previous qualifications in a particular subject or at a specified standard," some of the M.St. programs are more restrictive. Some require applicants to possess certain professional qualifications and work experience or to hold a completed undergraduate degree. For other M.St. programs, however, you may gain admission by demonstrating what ICE describes as "other evidence of capability to complete a Master's degree." The validity of such "other evidence" is judged by ICE officers on a case by case basis.

## How to Apply

Admission and course requirements vary significantly among the different programs. All the programs are geared toward "mature" students; however, there is no minimum age requirement or restriction. You should log on to www.ice.cam.ac.uk/mst/prospective-mst-students#mst-programmes, where you will find informational links to each program.

Most of the master of studies programs require the University of Cambridge standard graduate admissions application form known as

GRADSAF, which can be downloaded from www.admin.cam.ac.uk/ offices/gradstud/prospec/apply/paper/index.html#2. The form is to be printed out, completed, and submitted by mail.

Some programs have quite specific and restrictive prerequisites:

- The program in applied criminology and police management is a professional course of study intended primarily for senior police officers with:
  - a 2:1 (or equivalent) undergraduate degree from a recognized university
  - three years' work experience
  - enthusiasm and aptitude for sustainability leadership
  - meet university requirements for written and spoken English
  - support from employer
- The program in applied criminology, penology and management is also a professional course of study offered to "senior managers working within the criminal justice system both in the United Kingdom and overseas."
- The program in interdisciplinary design for the built environment is restricted to "individuals who have at least 3 years experience from all built environment disciplines."
- The program in sustainability leadership requires an undergraduate degree "from a recognised University," three years' work experience, and support from one's employer.

Other programs are *far* more open. For example:

- The international relations program admits students in alternate years and is restricted to forty students, who become full members of a Cambridge college. The course is taught during eight "intense residential weeks" spread over four periods during the first year and two short residential periods in the second year. A 25,000-word dissertation is required. Housing is available during the residential periods.

Applicants are expected to have an undergraduate degree earned with a GPA of 3.7. If you don't have high grades or have not completed an undergraduate degree, you can instead elect to "produce evidence of relevant and equivalent experience and [your] fitness to read for a Master's degree." In addition, you are required to provide degree transcripts, two academic or work-related references, and a thesis proposal, which is considered "an important element in the admissions process." No essay is required for admission.

- The local and regional history program admits twenty students in alternate years, so, like the international relations program, it accommodates forty students total. The program does not *require* applicants to have completed a bachelor's degree, but "successful applicants" are expected to have achieved a "first-year degree" from a UK university, an advanced diploma from the Institute of Continuing Education itself, or—most significant for U.S. students—"other evidence" of suitability to undertake study at the master's level. (ICE offers advanced diplomas in archaeology, historic environment, history of art, local history, and the study of religion. If you are interested in working toward this prerequisite, log on to www.ice.cam.ac.uk/certificates-and-diplomas for further information.) You will also need to submit a dissertation proposal, critique a historical document, and interview in person.

- The M.St. program in the study of Jewish-Christian relations combines religious, biblical, philosophical, and cultural studies with history, political science, and international relations. It is a two-year program that requires completion of a dissertation. Students have the option of entering "Track A," in which teaching is by traditional face-to-face methods that include lectures, seminars, and individual tutorials, or "Track B," which employs online learning. Students are admitted every year, and the program is taught jointly by the Centre for the Study of Jewish-Christian Relations, the Institute of Continuing Education, and the Faculty of Divinity. Those wishing to apply should contact the courses registrar directly.

## TUITION AND HOUSING

Tuition rates vary according to program, and the fee structure can be complex. For authoritative and timely information, you must contact the courses registrar directly.

Housing is available to M.St. students in Madingley Hall, which ICE officials describe as "an attractive house dating back to the mid-sixteenth century. The decoration of the Saloon and the formal Stair Hall was carried out 200 years later, and the whole fabric was renovated with great care around 1900. About five miles from the centre of Cambridge, the Hall stands in several acres of well-maintained gardens and overlooks a landscape which has changed relatively little since it was laid out by Capability Brown." Although the Institute of Continuing Education promises to meet the needs of students with disabilities, it does not guarantee to accommodate requests for particular rooms or facilities.

For more information, contact:

University of Cambridge
Institute of Continuing Education
Madingley Hall
Madingley, Cambridge CB23 8AQ
United Kingdom
+44 (0)1954 280399
Fax: +44 (0)1954 280200
Website: www.ice.cam.ac.uk

Courses Registrar
+44 (0)1223 746262
Email: registration@ice.cam.ac.uk

# 11

## Grabbing the Brass Rat at MIT

> ■ **KEYBOX**
>
> **SCHOOL:** Massachusetts Institute of Technology
>
> **LOCATION:** Cambridge, Massachusetts
>
> **COLLEGE RANKING:** 6
>
> **GATE POSITION:** Ajar
>
> **SAT REQUIRED:** Yes
>
> **HOUSING:** Yes
>
> **MINIMUM AGE:** 18 (24 for Davis Degree Program)
>
> **APPLICATION CRITERIA:** High
>
> **MEDIAN STARTING SALARY:** $71,100
>
> **COST COMPARED TO FRONT GATEWAY:** More (3+2 program)

The MIT mascot is a beaver informally and universally called Tim, who is featured prominently on the massive class ring that a student committee redesigns each year. As the engineer of the animal world, the beaver is an apt emblem for one of the world's preeminent schools of technology and engineering, but somebody at some time in years past decided that the beaver on the ring looked more like a rat and, ever since, the ring has been known as the "Brass Rat."

No one wore it more proudly than Trisha, who graduated from MIT a few years before starting her own small but successful Silicon Valley software firm. There was a time when she no more imagined herself joining the student ranks of MIT than she saw herself leading her own firm. She alternately struggled and dawdled through high school, earning good but unspectacular grades and spending far more time hacking computer games than studying in the library. She knew about MIT. In fact, it was the only school that got her intellectual juices flowing. However, with her grades—and her generally nonacademic "attitude"—college seemed out of the question, let alone a school as prestigious and demanding as MIT.

Trisha went from high school to the customer service desk of the local electronics chain store. Bright as she was, she soon found herself on an assistant manager's track, but after several years of untangling power cords she decided to take a long look at her dream school. She accepted the fact that she couldn't make it through the front gateway—not only because she hadn't been a high school standout, but because she was now well into her mid-twenties and no longer prime freshman material. Undaunted, she poked around until she found a little-known portal via Wellesley College, an institution few people would mention in the same sentence with MIT. It proved to be her way in.

## MIT TODAY

In 1861, the legislature of the Commonwealth of Massachusetts approved a petition for incorporation of the "Massachusetts Institute of Technology and Boston Society of Natural History," which was proposed by William Barton Rogers. A pioneer of higher education in the United States, Rogers believed that existing colleges and universities were inadequate to meet the challenges and exploit the opportunities presented by rapidly advancing nineteenth-century science and technology. He designed the so-called Rogers Plan, modeled on existing German research universities, in which faculty members divided their time between advanced research and seminar- and laboratory-based teaching.

The Civil War delayed the opening of MIT until 1865. Although its setting was urban—the first classes were held in downtown Boston— the Institute was eligible to receive funding from the 1862 Morrill Land-Grant Colleges Act because its mission was, in part, "to promote the liberal and practical education of the industrial classes." Today, along with Cornell University, MIT is one of only two private land- grant universities in the United States. The Institute used its funding to build a campus in Boston's Back Bay in 1866. Early in the twentieth century, George Eastman, creator of the Eastman Kodak Company, funded initial construction on MIT's present site on the Cambridge side of the Charles River. The Institute began occupying its new build- ings in 1916.

During the 1930s, under the leadership of President Karl Taylor Compton and Vice President Vannevar Bush—at the time one of the nation's most famous and most influential scientists—MIT revised its curriculum to put less emphasis on "industrial" applied science and more on "pure" sciences, especially physics and chemistry. This cata- pulted the Institute to the forefront of American science campuses.

Ranked number six nationally by *U.S. News & World Report*'s *Best Colleges 2013*, MIT has long been known as an incubator of hard-core scientific breakthroughs and civilization-changing technological ad- vances.

In 2009 alone, MIT invested $718.2 million in research activities, and as of 2011, the Institute was propelled by a $9.9 billion endowment overall (as of fiscal 2010). Since World War II, the federal government has been the largest single source of MIT's sponsored research, and the Institute employs some 3,500 researchers in addition to its regular fac- ulty. Together, in 2009, researchers and faculty disclosed 530 inven- tions, filed 184 patent applications, and received 166 patents, earning $136.3 million in royalties and other patent-related income. MIT re- search has produced such fundamental technological innovations as radar, magnetic core memory, single-electron transistors, and inertial guidance controls. MIT computer scientists have been responsible for major advances in cybernetics, artificial intelligence, computer languages, machine learning, robotics, and cryptography. MIT physics faculty members have collectively accumulated eight Nobel Prizes, four Dirac Medals, and three Wolf Prizes, which have made the Institute famous as a center for subatomic and quantum theory. While MIT chemists have earned three Nobel Prizes, biology faculty members have garnered six. Biologist Eric Lander, a Rhodes Scholar and MIT professor, was at the forefront of the epoch-making Human Genome Project.

While MIT is best known for science and engineering, it is also gaining a reputation as an innovative center for work in the humanities, arts, and social sciences. Five Nobel Prizes have been awarded to MIT economists. Linguist Noam Chomsky, cocreator of the concept and methods of generative grammar, is a professor in MIT's Department of Linguistics and Philosophy.

The 168-acre MIT campus, spanning a mile of the north rim of the Charles River basin in Cambridge, boasts a combination of stately collegiate edifices and examples of cutting-edge architecture. Among the latter are the MIT Media Lab, designed by architect I. M. Pei, in which researchers produce innovative uses of computer technology, and Frank Gehry's stunning Stata Center, which houses the Computer Science and Artificial Intelligence Laboratory as well as the Department of Linguistics and Philosophy. The campus is also home to one of the largest university-based nuclear reactors in the United States and maintains as well a pressurized wind tunnel for testing aeronautical designs and a towing tank for testing designs of ships and ocean structures. Research at MIT is not just for the senior scientists. There are a number of remarkable opportunities available to all MIT students, including the unique and popular Undergraduate Research Opportunities Program (UROP), which allows undergraduates to collaborate directly with faculty members. More than 70 percent of the student body participates in the program, and many students publish journal articles, file patent applications, and even launch start-up companies based on their UROP experiences.

## THE FIERCELY COMPETITIVE FRONT GATEWAY

MIT alumni, who hold twenty-seven Nobel Prizes collectively, include the likes of former U.N. Secretary General Kofi Annan, NASA astronaut Buzz Aldrin, Federal Reserve chairman Ben Bernanke, and the founders of Intel, McDonnell Douglas, Texas Instruments, and Rockwell International. It will come as no surprise, therefore, that the Institute is extraordinarily selective when it comes to admissions. With 4,384 undergraduates enrolled in 2012, MIT accepted a mere 9.7 percent of its total applicants. Even more daunting is that 95 percent of these applicants ranked in the top tenth of their high school classes, and none were below the top quarter. Incoming SAT scores were also predominantly at the highest end of the range.

## MIT'S BACK GATEWAY

Don't give up—at least not if you are female. For, as Trisha discovered, there *is* a back gateway into MIT.

The Institute offers a five-year dual-degree program via Wellesley College, a private women's liberal arts school. The program works this way: You must first be enrolled as a Wellesley student. Next, you must apply at Wellesley for candidacy in the 3/2 "double-degree program." Your application will be reviewed by a Wellesley committee, and if you are accepted, the committee will endorse your application to MIT as a transfer student. The application process unfolds in the spring semester of the sophomore year, and if accepted by MIT, you enroll there at the end of your junior year at Wellesley. Thus you will spend three years at Wellesley and two at MIT. Students graduate with degrees from both Wellesley College and MIT.

Important restrictions apply to the transfer. Only the following departments (known at MIT as "courses") are open to students coming from Wellesley:

- Architecture (Course 4)
- Urban studies and planning (Course 11)
- Aeronautics and astronautics (Course 16)
- Biological engineering (Course 20)
- Chemical engineering (Course 10)
- Civil and environmental engineering (Course 1)
- Electrical engineering and computer science (Course 6)
- Materials science and engineering (Course 3)
- Mechanical engineering (Course 2)
- Nuclear engineering (Course 22)

To ensure that you complete all MIT prerequisites before actually transferring, both Wellesley and MIT will assign major advisors who will help you plan an appropriate sequence. Having completed your third year at Wellesley, you will move on to a fourth and fifth year at MIT; however, the Wellesley/MIT Exchange Program permits cross-registration throughout the entire five-year period, so that you may actually integrate the two study programs extensively.

## TUITION AND HOUSING

The first three years are governed by Wellesley College financial and financial aid policies, whereas the last two are governed by those of MIT. Although tuition at both institutions is about the same ($41,824 at Wellesley and $40,732 at MIT in 2012), the availability of financial aid may differ significantly. You will want to investigate and consider this. Also be aware that you will be paying for five, not four, years of undergraduate education.

The dorm fee for undergrads at MIT is a little over $12,000 but depends on the specific housing and dining arrangements you select. The Wellesley College room fee is around $6,500, and the meal plan costs about the same. So the room and board is about the same at both.

## How to Apply

You will need to begin preparing early at Wellesley to ensure that you complete the science core courses required by MIT, which include sequences in calculus, physics, and additional sciences.

If you are already attending Wellesley and are interested in the double-degree program, schedule a meeting with the class dean and a Wellesley-designated professor to explore your options. You will also need to ensure that you take the appropriate preparatory courses and (according to the Wellesley website) "become familiar with prospective departments at MIT by talking with faculty members there and by taking at least one course at MIT."

During the fall of your sophomore year, you must contact the transfer admissions office at MIT to request an application. Next, you must complete the Application for Wellesley Support and submit it to the class dean by January 15 of your sophomore year. A committee will review your application and "indicate to MIT its support for the candidacy of an applicant appropriate for this program." The full transfer application is due to MIT by February 15 of your sophomore year. In addition to Wellesley's support, you will be asked to write an essay and furnish three letters of recommendation, including at least one from an MIT faculty member. MIT announces acceptances by about April 1.

## THE COLLEGE OF HILLARY CLINTON
## AND DIANE SAWYER

What if you are not yet enrolled at Wellesley?

Founded in the Boston suburb of Wellesley, Massachusetts, in 1870, Wellesley College enrolls about 2,300 undergraduates, all of whom are women. It is an academically challenging institution, which shaped the minds of Hillary Clinton, Diane Sawyer, and many other female leaders. In its 2013 edition of *Best Colleges*, *U.S. News & World Report* ranked Wellesley number six among liberal arts colleges in the United States. Its suburban Boston campus is both wooded and picturesque.

Wellesley is rated as "most selective" by *U.S. News*, which reported that in 2012 the college accepted 30.9 percent of applicants. The odds of a qualified female student getting into Wellesley are therefore nearly four times better than they are for that same student gaining admission directly into MIT. Of course, you still have to be accepted by MIT as a transfer student, but with Wellesley's support, that acceptance rate is generally high.

## WELLESLEY'S BACK GATEWAY

Although it is easier to enter Wellesley by the front gateway than it is to enter MIT the same way, Wellesley offers its own back gateway. Called the Davis Degree Program, it is geared for women who are older than the "traditional" college age. Applicants must be at least twenty-four and must not have completed a bachelor's degree elsewhere. "Davis Scholars," as accepted applicants are known, take the same classes as other students, participate in the same organizations and activities, and live on campus if they choose.

## Applying to the Davis Degree Program

To apply for the Davis Degree Program—without application fee!—you will be asked to complete three forms online (see www.wellesley.edu/admission/davisapp/instructions.html):

Part I: The Wellesley College Supplement
Part II: The Common Application for Transfer Students
Part III: The Davis Degree Program Supplement

In addition, you will need to submit:

An official high school transcript or GED scores
Official transcripts from all colleges and universities you have attended
Three letters of recommendation
A transfer credit form (available online) if you are applying for transfer credit
An up-to-date résumé
Official course descriptions and a statement of degree requirements for all courses for which you expect to receive transfer credit

You will also be asked to an interview, which you may arrange at any time during the year, provided that it takes place at least two weeks before the admission application deadline of March 1. If you live far from campus, you may arrange an off-campus interview with a Wellesley alumna who lives closer to your home.

For more information on the Davis Degree Program, visit http://web.wellesley.edu/web/Admission/Apply/HowTo/DavisApply.

For general information concerning both MIT and Wellesley, contact:

Massachusetts Institute of Technology
Admissions Office
Website: www.mitadmissions.org
Email: admissions@mit.edu

Wellesley College
Board of Admission
106 Central Street
Wellesley, MA 02481-8203
(781) 283-2270
Website: www.wellesley.edu
Email: admission@wellesley.edu

The Elisabeth Kaiser Davis Degree Program
Continuing Education House
Wellesley College
106 Central Street
Wellesley, MA 02481
(781) 283-2665
Website: www.wellesley.edu/advising/davis
Email: admission@wellesley.edu

# 12

# New Ivy Among the Magnolias: Emory University

■ **KEYBOX**

SCHOOL: Emory University

LOCATION: Atlanta, Georgia

COLLEGE RANKING: 20

GATE POSITION: Wide open

SAT REQUIRED: Yes

HOUSING: Yes

MINIMUM AGE: 18

APPLICATION CRITERIA: Moderate

MEDIAN STARTING SALARY: $50,600

COST COMPARED TO FRONT GATEWAY: Less

Abigail loved growing up on the farm, but she didn't want her future bounded by the broad horizons of rural Indiana. She thought of attending a great university in a big city on the East Coast, and with her impressive 3.9 GPA and above-average SAT scores, her high school guidance counselor encouraged her to apply to several of the Ivy League schools. Yet, as she thought about it, cities like New York and Boston seemed a little harsh to her. Yes, she wanted something big, but also a little softer, perhaps. Besides, as the oldest child of six, she knew her family would be hard-pressed to fund four years of Ivy League tuition, even with financial aid. And she also knew that even a lofty GPA and "very good" SATs might still not be enough to get her into Harvard or Columbia, especially coming, as she did, from a rural Indiana public high school.

In her senior year, she started reading good things about Emory in Atlanta, a big Southeastern city that appealed to her more than the larger (and colder) cities of the Northeast. While Emory was still highly selective, it accepted at least a third of those who applied, and Abigail was confident she had the grades, test scores, and recommendations to get in. Trouble was that Emory tuition is even higher than Harvard's. But Abigail wasn't dismayed for long. She soon discovered an economical back gateway to Emory University, one of the best schools in the nation.

## OASIS IN AN URBAN SETTING

Emory was ranked twentieth among national universities by *U.S. News & World Report* in *Best Colleges 2013* and has been hailed as one of the "New Ivies" by *Newsweek* magazine. With an annual acceptance rate of 26.7 percent, this school receives a flood of applications each year from students eager to take advantage of a rigorous curriculum on a uniquely beautiful campus. Its core, the original seventy-two acres acquired when the school was expanded in 1914 from its origins as Emory *College*—founded at Oxford, Georgia, in 1836—was designed by the great landscape architect Frederick Law Olmsted. Like Olmsted's better known masterpiece, New York City's Central Park, the campus, now grown to more than 740 acres in Atlanta's scenic Druid Hills neighborhood, combines "wild" with "manicured" elements that make it a truly bucolic oasis in an urban setting.

The campus is located adjacent to the U.S. Centers for Disease Control and Prevention (CDC) and the American Cancer Society, as part of a scientific and medical complex known as the Clifton Corridor, which includes eight of Emory's own nine affiliated hospitals, the university's medical school, and a world-renowned primate research center. Emory medical faculty are, among other things, leaders in HIV/AIDS research, treatment, and prevention, having developed two commonly used AIDS drug therapies. The medical school also operates one of the largest academic vaccine centers in the world.

Emory University prides itself on being a leader in environmental sustainability, with more square feet of LEED-certified green building space than any other campus in America. A sustainable food initiative aims to put food grown on campus and purchased from local agricultural sources into dining halls. Campus shuttles run on alternative fuel, including biodiesel produced by the cooking oil used in student cafeterias.

In addition to its medical school and premed preparation, Emory is renowned for superb law, business, and theology schools, as well as for excellent programs in the humanities, one of the highlights of which is archaeology; the campus is home to the small but magnificent Michael Carlos Museum, which houses the South's finest collection of Egyptian, Greek, Roman, African, and pre-classical antiquities.

In 2012, Emory had 7,441 full-time undergraduate students enrolled in sixty-six majors, fifty-three minors, seventeen joint concentrations, and ten interdepartmental programs leading to a bachelor's degree. The most popular majors are business, economics, political science, psychology, and biology. Undergraduate education takes place at the Emory College of Arts and Sciences, the Goizueta Business School, the Neil Hodgson Woodruff School of Nursing, and—as we will see shortly—Oxford College. Graduate programs are offered at the James T. Laney School of Graduate Studies, the School of Law, the School of Medicine, the Rollins School of Public Health, and the Candler School of Theology, in addition to the Goizueta Business School and the Woodruff School of Nursing.

Splendidly endowed Emory—$5.4 billion as of 2012—has five libraries that hold a total of 3.1 million volumes in addition to many thousands of digital information resources. Atlanta and the Druid Hills neighborhood offer a myriad of dining, cultural, and sports opportunities in addition to shopping attractions that draw visitors from all over the South.

## EMORY'S BACK GATEWAY

Emory University turns away 70 percent of those who come to call at its front gateway. Those who *are* accepted face the challenge of financing an education that, for the academic year 2012–2013, cost $42,980 in tuition and fees and $12,000 for room and board (52.1 percent of students received need-based financial aid that fully met their need).

Just thirty-eight miles east of Emory's front gateway, is the *original* Emory, which is now named Oxford College, after its picturesque hometown. Today, Oxford College is officially one of the nine academic divisions of Emory University. It is a small campus with about nine hundred students, all freshmen and sophomores, who enjoy a seventeen-to-one student-to-instructor ratio. After successfully completing their sophomore year in an intensive liberal arts program, students are automatically enrolled as juniors in the Emory College of Arts and Sciences (unless they wish to compete with other applicants to enter Emory's nursing or business schools) and leave the town of Oxford—population 1,892—for the city of Atlanta, the metropolitan population of which is nearly five and a half million.

Why would you want to enter Emory through the Oxford back gateway?

Whereas Emory's Atlanta campus accepts less than a third of those who apply, Oxford, in 2012, accepted 41 percent—and, in the process, saved those it accepted significant money. In 2012, a year at Oxford College cost $5,738 *less* in tuition plus room and board than that same academic year spent at Emory University in Atlanta.

## MORE THAN JUST A BACK DOOR

Significantly raising the likelihood of getting in and getting a 9 percent discount on the first two years of a college education are compelling reasons for entering Emory via Oxford College, but many students choose this alternative not because they *have* to but because they *want* to. Although typical class sizes are not much bigger at Emory than they are at Oxford College—nineteen students versus seventeen—Emory *is* a university, with a vast campus in a big city and a combined under-graduate/graduate student body of 13,893 in 2012. Oxford College, by contrast, is an intimate college environment—fifty-six acres in a small Georgia town—and emphasizes teaching and personal interaction with professors. Many students find such an environment the perfect transition from high school to university.

With "teaching . . . the major focus at Oxford . . . our students rave about the connections they form with their professors." As the college website goes on to explain, "What sets Oxford apart from many other schools is the fact that we are focused exclusively on the first two years and can concentrate on the transformative potential of this phase of baccalaureate education."

Students who go on from Oxford College to Emory's Atlanta campus are called "continuees" rather than "transferees." By all accounts, they are accepted as full members of the university community and are even offered special assistance, if needed, to ease the transition from small-town campus to big-city university life.

If there is a downside to this back gateway, we can't find it. Never-theless, you do need to understand that your junior and senior years will be governed by Emory University tuition and room-and-board rates, which, as of 2012, were 9 percent higher than those charged by Oxford College.

## How to Apply

To apply to Oxford College in order to gain entrance into Emory University, you need first to complete Emory University's Common Application Supplement, which you can find online by logging on to www .commonapp.org/CommonApp/default.aspx. This document contains important information about application options and deadlines.

After completing and submitting the supplement, you must fill out the Common Application itself, which is available at the same website. A $50 application fee is required and may be paid online by credit card or by mail with a check or money order. Note that you may simultaneously apply to both Oxford College and directly to Emory College, if you like. You will only pay one application fee for both divisions.

You will be asked to furnish official transcripts for all high schools and colleges attended, as well as SAT or ACT scores, which may be reported directly by your high school or the testing service. Unless you have been homeschooled, the SAT II is not required. Although you must complete the essay section of the SAT, the school considers only the Critical Reading and Math sections of the test for admission and notes that the "essay section is currently being used for research only."

Oxford College requires only one recommendation, from your high school guidance counselor. Your counselor may write a letter or simply complete the Common Application Secondary School Report Form online. Although this is the only absolutely *required* recommendation, the college encourages you to submit up to two teacher recommendations as well. These may also be in the form of letters, or your teachers may complete the Common Application Teacher Evaluation.

The Common Application will ask you to list all of your awards and distinctions as well as significant extracurricular activities, which "include anything you are involved in at your school or in your community." Admissions officers explain that there is "no magic number for activities. Some students are involved in many things and others dedicate their time to only one or two activities. We are simply looking for well-rounded students who want to contribute to our community at Oxford." In addition, you will be asked to list your favorite books, recordings, movies, sources of news and other information, websites, and even keepsakes, and to share two adjectives that your peers would use to describe you.

The application includes an essay section, which the Oxford admissions officers describe as "your chance to show us who you really are. We want to get to know you beyond the nuts and bolts of your application and transcript." They explain that they do not read the essay for grammar, but caution that "it should be well written and proofread carefully." The essay should be one to two pages long and must address one of five topics:

1. Why is Oxford a good match for you?
2. What talent, accomplishment, or pursuit has given you the greatest joy or satisfaction?
3. Discuss some issue of personal, local, national, or international concern and its importance.
4. Describe a person, character in fiction, historical figure, or creative work and explain their influence.
5. Please describe a daily routine or tradition of yours that may seem ordinary to others but holds significance to you.

Naturally, academic performance plays a central role in your acceptance to Oxford College. As the school explains, "To be competitive for admission, you should have taken a rigorous course load, based on what is offered at your school. If your school offers honors, AP, IB or other types of advanced coursework, we would like to see that you have taken advantage of some of these classes."

The application deadline is November 15 for early action, February 1 for regular decision for the upcoming fall semester, and December 1 for regular decision for the upcoming spring semester.

## TUITION AND HOUSING

On its website, Oxford College announces its commitment to "the philosophy that the cost of a college education should not be a deterrent to prospective students. Recognizing that in today's economy, paying for an education is a challenge, we encourage all students to apply for financial aid, whether or not they think they are eligible." Remember, Oxford College tuition is 9 percent less than tuition at Emory University, which means that you will receive a substantial discount toward your Emory diploma during the first two years of your undergraduate education.

Unlike some other back gateways, Oxford College encourages all students to live and eat on campus. Residence halls are staffed by professional as well as student advisors, who will help you to navigate your first two years of college life. The school puts a premium value on creating and maintaining a sense of community and invites students to regularly dine with faculty in the campus dining hall, which is known affectionately as Lil's. This is just one of many "opportunities to interact with one another, become leaders in your community, and attend both social and educational programs" that the college endeavors to offer its students.

For more information, contact:

Emory University
201 Dowman Drive
Atlanta, GA 30322
(404) 727-6036
Website: www.emory.edu
Email: admiss@emory.edu

Oxford College
100 Hamill Street
Oxford, GA 30054
(770) 784-8888
Website: www.oxford.emory.edu

# 13

# Regional Presence, National Reputation: Washington University in St. Louis

Although he had left college years earlier, without graduating, David found success as a businessman and was making a very comfortable living. But after sixteen years of nine-to-five, he had begun to yearn for more. He confessed to being a Sunday painter, and now he wanted to take some time, buckle down, and earn a degree in fine arts.

What college he'd had, it seemed to him, was a lifetime ago, and he wondered if he was simply too old to get back into the game, but when he mentioned his aspirations one day during a business lunch, a col-league pointed him to Washington University. A longtime resident of the St. Louis suburbs, David knew that these days Washington was practically in the Ivy League. His eyes lit up for a moment, but then, thanking his lunch partner for the advice, he remarked, "I've been away from school so long, they'll never let me in the front gate."

"Then why not try the back?" his friend suggested.

## FROM LOCAL NIGHT SCHOOL
## TO TOP NATIONAL UNIVERSITY

Washington University was founded in 1853 thanks to the efforts of a group of St. Louis religious, political, and business leaders who were motivated by the conviction that the lower Midwest should have a major institution of higher learning. While most great American pri-vate universities came into existence through the sponsorship of a reli-gious denomination or because of the endowment of some visionary benefactor, Washington University was born of a community leader-ship coalition and, as such, struggled financially through its early years. Nevertheless, its leaders persevered and created an important regional school.

At first, Washington University was primarily a night school, serv-ing a mostly working population in downtown St. Louis. In 1867, the university's law school came into being—the first private nonsectarian law school west of the Mississippi. It was not until 1882, however, that Washington University became a university in the truest sense of the word, when it expanded into various departments and moved into a number of buildings. The now famous School of Medicine was founded in 1891, following the affiliation of the existing St. Louis Medical Col-lege with the university.

The transformation of Washington University from a regional school to an institution of national reputation began in 1922 when physics professor Arthur Holly Compton discovered, during research he conducted at the university, the "Compton Effect," which demonstrated the particle concept of electromagnetic radiation and is a cornerstone of modern nuclear physics. This work earned Compton the Nobel Prize in physics for 1927 and helped put the university on the map. Compton subsequently joined the physics faculty of the University of Chicago, but he returned to Washington University in 1946 as its chancellor.

At present, Washington University in St. Louis consists of eleven schools and colleges:

College of Arts and Sciences
School of Engineering
School of Law
College of Art
School of Medicine
College of Architecture
Olin Business School
Graduate School of Arts and Sciences
George Warren Brown School of Social Work
Sam Fox School of Design and Visual Arts
University College

Undergraduates enroll in one or more of five of these schools, including the College of Arts and Sciences, the College of Architecture, the College of Art, the Olin Business School, and the School of Engineering. With its especially strong medical school, Washington University in St. Louis draws many premed students, who concentrate in the natural sciences, particularly biology and chemistry. The Washington University Medical Center spans a dozen city blocks and is home to the medical school and renowned teaching hospitals—Barnes-Jewish Hospital and St. Louis Children's Hospital—as well as a cancer center, education center, and the Central Institute for the Deaf.

The heart of any great university is its library. Washington University has fourteen of them, making it Missouri's largest library system, with more than 4.2 million volumes. In addition to the main Olin Library, there are separate specialty libraries, including the Kranzberg Art and Architecture Library, the Business Library, the Chemistry Library, the East Asian Library, the Law Library, the Becker Medical Library, the Music Library, the Physics Library, the Social Work Library, the Special Collections and Archives, and the West Campus Library. The campus also features the Mildred Lane Kemper Art Museum, established in 1881, which houses artworks from U.S. and European artists, ranging from Rembrandt to Rauschenberg.

With research a central focus of the university since the early 1920s, most faculty members are actively engaged in advanced projects. Some 60 percent of undergraduates participate in this faculty research, which is often of a strongly interdisciplinary nature. The Center for Measuring University Performance (http://mup.asu.edu/) has named the school one of the top ten private research universities in the nation, and Washington University regularly receives major funding from the National Institutes of Health (NIH), the Department of Defense, the National Science Foundation (NSF), and NASA.

The emphasis on research is never allowed to come at the expense of teaching, both inside the classroom and out. Students are offered free writing advice and support at the university's dedicated writing center. There is also career planning assistance, including numerous workshops and referrals. The Center for Advanced Learning, known more familiarly as Cornerstone, offers a host of "collaborative learning opportunities," among which are facilitated study groups, workshops, and help sessions for specific courses as well as one-on-one academic mentoring. Peer mentors are assigned to each dorm, and evening help desks are also available in residences. All students are invited to take advantage of academic coaching, study skills assistance, and professional assessment of individual learning styles. In addition to peer mentoring, undergraduates enjoy broad access to one-on-one mentoring relationships with top faculty. Last but hardly least, every student (and faculty member, for that matter) is entitled to free mass transit passes that help open up culturally diverse St. Louis to all.

## "MOST SELECTIVE"

Today, this prosperous institution has achieved lofty status among the nation's universities, ranked fourteenth by *U.S. News & World Report* in *Best Colleges 2013*. Washington University offers nineteen undergraduate majors that together are considered among the top ten major programs in the United States. The school's global rankings include placing at number thirty in the 2010 Academic Ranking of World Universities by Shanghai's Jiao Tong University (a ranking based on the quality of scientific research leading toward a Nobel Prize) and number thirty-eight in the *Times* (London) Higher Education World University Rankings.

With its dramatic rise in national recognition, the university has experienced explosive growth in applications, receiving in 2012 record-breaking undergraduate applications, of which 16.5 percent were accepted.

## THE BACK GATEWAY

With demand for places in Washington University now so intense, 83.5 percent of applicants are turned away at the front gateway. Fortunately, way back in 1854, the institution developed an evening program intended to accommodate the waves of foreign immigrants who were pouring into St. Louis and who were in need of what was then referred to as "industrial training." The night school was called University College and originally offered English language training and basic general education courses. Today, University College provides for students of all ages the back gateway to Washington University's College of Arts and Sciences. Both day and evening classes are offered—though tuition for the daytime classes is higher—and students can earn undergraduate as well as graduate degrees.

As with most other back gateways to elite universities, a degree earned at University College is identical to a degree earned elsewhere within the Washington University system. University College offers a range of academic opportunities that should appeal to nearly every interest. Areas of study include majors in anthropology, communications, journalism, English, mathematics, political science, psychology, liberal arts, and creative writing.

## How to Apply

Before you submit your application, you are encouraged to contact the University College Office of Admissions and Student Services at (314) 935-6777 to discuss your academic goals and interests. Basic requirements for admission to a degree program include:

- A high school diploma or GED
- A minimum of twelve credits of college-level course work with a minimum GPA of 2.7, or
- If you have no college credit work, a high school transcript plus SAT or ACT scores.

In addition, you must submit:

- An essay describing your educational goals and your work experience
- Official transcripts of all previous college work

You will also be asked to "indicate any other factors which you think should be taken into consideration relating to your application for admission."

## TUITION AND HOUSING

Tuition for University College courses is charged per credit unit and varies according to your chosen course of study. Current tuition schedules and financial aid information are available at the University College website (http://ucollege.wustl.edu/tuition/tuition_fees). Note that, for 2012–2013, tuition ranged from $605 to $710 per credit unit for undergraduates. Since most bachelor's degree programs require about 120 units of course work, you can expect to pay in the neighborhood of $70,000 for study culminating in a degree. This isn't cheap, but consider that, in 2012–2013, tuition and fees for front gateway students was $43,705 per academic year (exclusive of room and board), which adds up to a four-year total of $174,820. At better than half off, University College seems like a bargain—and, as it is for "regular" students (41 percent of whom received aid in 2011–2012), financial aid is available to University College students.

Of course, you will still have to meet living expenses in addition to your tuition. For front gateway students, room and board cost $13,580 in 2012–2013. Except during the summer term, no university housing is available to University College students; however, the St. Louis area, including the neighborhood adjacent to the university, offers a wide range of places to live with expenses comparable to or even below the cost of university-provided accommodations. (Washington University's Office of Residential Life does offer on-campus housing for students who are enrolled in summer courses, so if you are planning to study over the summer, you may secure dormitory accommodations.)

For more information, contact:

University College
Washington University

Campus Box 1085
One Brookings Drive
St. Louis, MO 63130
(800) 638-0700
Website: www.wustl.edu
Email: admissions@wustl.edu

# 14

# In the Research Triangle: Duke University

Ever since she was a little girl, Jessica had been a great planner. Whatever the game, the task, the project, she decided on her goal, then decided on exactly what she had to do to reach it. As far back as middle school, she set her sights on Duke University, after her uncle, an alum, filled her head with stories of what a great place it was. Armed with her goal, she made her plan, which included getting straight A's in high school and earning a set of SAT scores well into the upper percentiles.

She planned her work, and she worked her plan. Then life blundered in to wreck it.

Late in Jessica's junior year, her mother was diagnosed with breast cancer. Jessica's world was not only thrown into a chaos of anxiety, she now directed all her energies to helping her mother—running errands, taking her to and from doctor's appointments, and generally being there for her through the ordeals of surgery, chemotherapy, and radiation. Because there was only so much of Jessica to go around, her grades began to slip, and the goal of a Duke education soon sunk below the horizon.

A year after the cancer diagnosis, Jessica's mother looked to be in full recovery mode. As relief replaced anxiety, Jessica's dreams of Duke resurfaced. But it was now clearly too late to repair the damage to her GPA.

Yet just as her mother hadn't given up when she was diagnosed, so Jessica decided to look for a way—*some* way, *any* way—to get her goal back within her grasp. She sat down with her high school counselor, and, together, they did some homework about Duke. Before long, they discovered a back gateway that seemed to have been made just for her.

## PART OF THE SOUTHEAST'S RESEARCH AND HIGH-TECH AREA

The north-central portion of the state of North Carolina—the Piedmont region—is home to three universities and a host of high-tech firms that, collectively, form the Southeast's celebrated "Research Triangle." Two of the schools, North Carolina State and the University of North Carolina, are state institutions, and one, Duke University, is private.

The eighth-ranked American university in the 2013 *U.S. News & World Report* survey, Duke started out humbly in 1838 as "Brown's Schoolhouse," founded by a society of Methodists and Quakers in the

Piedmont village of Trinity. The state legislature recognized the school with a charter in 1841, and Brown's Schoolhouse was renamed the Union Institute Academy that year. A decade later, in 1851, it became Normal College, a teacher's college, and in 1859, in recognition of the financial contribution of the Methodist Church, it was renamed Trinity College.

Sleepy and sedate, Trinity College weathered the Civil War and earned a fine local reputation that motivated North Carolina tobacco barons—and faithful Methodists—Washington Duke and Julian S. Carr to finance both an enlargement and a move to the city of Durham in 1892. Four years after the move, in 1896, Washington Duke presented Trinity College with a $100,000 endowment, on condition that it admit women "on an equal footing with men." The new location and the generous funding advanced Trinity from local repute to regional renown, and in 1924, James B. Duke, Washington's son, created the $40 million Duke Endowment, which funded a number of charitable institutions and four colleges, including Trinity. In recognition of the gift, Trinity's president, William Preston Few, persuaded Duke to allow the college—now prepared to assume university status—to be named after him. Duke agreed, on condition that it would be recognized as a memorial to his father rather than himself.

Duke fashioned its first national identity with its engineering program and established a separate school of engineering in 1939. During the 1960s, the university stepped more fully into the national spotlight when it became a progressive focus for the civil rights movement, and at the end of the decade, with the ascension of former North Carolina governor Terry Sanford to the presidency, the creation of the Fuqua School of Business, the opening of the magnificent William R. Perkins Library (resources today include nearly six million volumes and 17.7 million manuscripts), and the founding of what would become the Sanford School of Public Policy, Duke began to draw enrollment applications from not only across the country but across the world.

Duke University researchers were the first to map the final human chromosome, and they pioneered studies in nonlinear dynamics, chaos, and complex systems in chaos. Notable alumni include Richard Nixon—a graduate of the university's esteemed School of Law—Melinda Gates, former General Motors chairman and CEO Rich Wagoner, Morgan Stanley CEO John J. Mack, former Pfizer chairman and CEO Edmund Pratt Jr., CBS News and Sports president Sean McManus, and talk show host Charlie Rose. Duke students routinely take courses from leading scientific, political, and literary figures, including Peter Agre, winner of the 2003 Nobel Prize in chemistry, former U.S. solicitor general Walter Dellinger III, and Chilean-American playwright and novelist Ariel Dorfman.

## SELECTIVITY

Duke University consists of ten schools:

- Trinity College of Arts and Sciences (established 1859)
- School of Law (1904)
- Divinity School (1926)
- Graduate School (1926)
- School of Medicine (1930)
- School of Nursing (1931)
- Pratt School of Engineering (1939)
- Fuqua School of Business (1969)
- Sanford School of Public Policy (1971)
- Nicholas School of the Environment (1991)

Undergraduates enroll either in Trinity or the Pratt School of Engineering, and admissions selectivity is on a par with that of Ivy League institutions. Ranked eighth overall by *U.S. News & World Report* in *Best Colleges 2013*—that's up from number nine in 2011—Duke is a "most selective" institution, which accepted 14 percent of applicants in 2012.

## DUKE'S BACK GATEWAY

Make no mistake, the Duke academic program is both rigorous and challenging, and, as with Ivy League schools, getting through the front gateway is no easy matter. Fortunately, there is a little-known back gateway alternative—two alternatives, in fact.

The Nicholas School of Environment, newest of Duke's ten colleges, having been founded in 1991, offers a "Cooperative College Program," which draws qualified students at other colleges and universities directly from three years of undergraduate study into a professional graduate track at Duke.

The one major condition of the Cooperative College Program is that you must want to earn one of two graduate degrees offered by the Nicholas School: the master of environmental management (M.E.M.) or the master of forestry (M.F.). While these are specialized and specific, they are also highly esteemed degrees that lead to eminently employable professions. Duke's medical, law, business, and engineering schools have long been recognized as among the best in the United States, and Duke's offerings in the natural sciences, most notably ecology, biology, and neuroscience, are also ranked near the top. More recently, the Nicholas School has earned Duke a place at the forefront of environmental training and research with an innovative and interdisciplinary approach to such issues as global warming and greenhouse gas pollution, ecosystem management and conservation, and human health and the environment. In 2007, Duke established the Nicholas School Gendell Center for Engineering, Energy, and the Environment, which was designed to provide research, instruction, and other resources to investigate causes of and find solutions to complex environmental issues. If environmental science interests you, the Nicholas School of the Environment is a great place to be.

## THE PROGRAMS

The master of forestry (M.F.) program offers a single professional degree in forest resource management (FRM), whereas the master of environmental management (M.E.M.) program currently allows specialization in one of seven areas:

- **Coastal Environmental Management (CEM)**—CEM trains "scientifically informed professionals to fill coastal policy and management, research, or advocacy positions in federal and state agencies, industry, consulting firms, and nonprofit organizations."
- **Ecosystem Science and Conservation (ESC)**—ESC "focuses on the natural science, policy, and management issues that relate to the stewardship of our natural resources."
- **Ecotoxicology and Environmental Health (EEH)**—EEH, which "emphasizes interactions among human/environmental health and ecological processes," qualifies graduates to work as environmental analysts or consultants in both the private and public sectors.
- **Energy and Environment (EE)**—EE provides "students with the skills and knowledge necessary to effectively address energy and environmental challenges."
- **Environmental Economics and Policy (EEP)**—EEP is "designed to train decision-makers, those who offer them expert advice, and those who try to influence policy through the political process."
- **Global Environmental Change (GEC)**—GEC "provides an integrated package of fundamental environmental science, analytical skills, and management and policy training," all designed for those who want "to develop a career in public, private, or nonprofit sectors."

- **Water and Air Resources (WAR)**—WAR focuses on the "physical, chemical, and biological processes affecting aquatic and atmospheric environments." Those who complete the WAR program may enter careers as analysts or consultants for firms and agencies concerned with the management and protection of water and air resources.

If the focus of the Nicholas programs strikes you as highly professional and even vocational, that is because it is. School officials report that 97 percent of M.E.M. graduates are placed in jobs with annual salaries ranging from $25,000 in the nonprofit sector to $75,000 in private industry, whereas those holding the M.F. degree can expect entry-level salaries of $31,000 to $42,000.

## THE COOPERATIVE COLLEGE PROGRAM: HOW IT WORKS

The Cooperative College Program is a 3/2 program, which reduces the usual six-year timeline for the bachelor's-master's degree sequence to just five years. For example, an undergraduate at Oglethorpe University in Atlanta, if accepted into either the M.E.M. or M.F. program, would study for three years at Oglethorpe and then transfer to Duke's Nicholas School. After completing his or her first year there, the student would receive a bachelor's degree. Then, after successfully completing a second year of study at Duke, he or she would be awarded the M.E.M. or M.F. degree.

The Environmental Program at Duke's Cooperative College is more than thirty-five years old and originally included "cooperating" agreements with approximately twenty-five liberal arts colleges on the East Coast. Today, that number exceeds eighty colleges and universities in every region of the country. Nevertheless, it is a small program. Only

1 to 2 percent of the Nicholas School's professional degree candidates are 3/2 students.

## How to Apply

The *Cooperative College Program Manual* makes it clear that there are "no guarantees" of admission into the program. "In all cases," the manual states, "applicants from cooperative institutions are evaluated on the same basis as other applicants to the school. . . . There is no guarantee that 3/2 applicants will be admitted to the school just as there is no guarantee of admissions for any student."

Specific prerequisites for admission include:

- Some training in the natural or social sciences related to the student's area of interest
- Calculus and statistics course work
- Undergraduate experience and training in professional writing

Some specializations require additional preparation. For example, microeconomics is a prerequisite for students planning to pursue degrees in EE, EEP, CEM, and FRM; moreover, students planning for a degree in FRM, ESC, or EEP must have completed at least one ecology course, and students pursuing EEH must successfully complete undergraduate courses in biology and chemistry. Other areas of specialization have their own requirements, and some of the cooperating undergraduate institutions also have requirements of their own.

The cooperating undergraduate institution will provide a designated advisor to assist you in planning your first three years of undergraduate work. In some schools, the advisor is a member of a relevant department—such as biology, botany, economics, or public policy—while, in other cooperating institutions, the advisor is a member of the undergraduate dean's staff.

Prospective 3/2 students must, like any other Duke applicant, apply by the February 1 deadline and should directly contact the Enrollment Services Office for application materials. The complete application consists of:

1. An application form
2. A personal statement, which should demonstrate your ability to handle graduate work and present your plans for graduate study as well as your plans for a career in natural resources
3. Three letters of recommendation
4. Two copies of transcripts from all academic institutions previously attended
5. Official GRE scores
6. A nonrefundable application fee of $75
7. A statement from the student's undergraduate dean that the student will be released to enroll in a 3/2 program
8. A résumé or CV (not required, but strongly encouraged)

All courses undertaken to meet program prerequisites must be taken for a grade, and you must earn a grade of B– or better in each course in order for it to count toward the prerequisite. Although program officials say that they judge applicants individually and disclaim any minimum GPA or GRE score as absolute admission prerequisites, it is true that most students successfully admitted to the program have had GPAs above 3.4 and GRE verbal scores of 600 and above, with quantitative scores of 650 or better and analytical scores of 500 or better.

As of 2012, cooperating colleges and universities participating in the program included:

Albion College, Albion, MI
Albright College, Reading, PA
Alfred University, Alfred, NY
Allegheny College, Meadville, PA
Armstrong State College, Savannah, GA

Assumption College, Worcester, MA
Augustana College, Rock Island, IL
Baker University, Baldwin City, KS
Baldwin-Wallace College, Berea, OH
Bard College, Annandale-on-Hudson, NY
Baylor University, Waco, TX
Beloit College, Beloit, WI
Birmingham-Southern College, Birmingham, AL
Bridgewater College, Bridgewater, VA
Butler University, Indianapolis, IN
Carson Newman College, Jefferson City, TN
Catawba College, Salisbury, NC
Christopher Newport University, Newport News, VA
College of Wooster, Wooster, OH
Colorado College, Colorado Springs, CO
Cornell College, Mount Vernon, IA
Denison University, Granville, OH
Dillard University, New Orleans, LA
Doane College, Crete, NE
Drew University, Madison, NJ
Elizabethtown College, Elizabethtown, PA
Emory and Henry College, Emory, VA
Florida Southern College, Lakeland, FL
Franklin & Marshall College, Lancaster, PA
Franklin College, Franklin, IN
Furman University, Greenville, SC
Gettysburg College, Gettysburg, PA
Guilford College, Greensboro, NC
Gustavus Adolphus College, Saint Peter, MN
Heidelberg College, Tiffin, OH
High Point University, High Point, NC
Hiram College, Hiram, OH
Illinois Wesleyan University, Bloomington, IL

Indiana University, Bloomington, IN
Juniata College, Huntington, PA
Kenyon College, Gambier, OH
Knox College, Galesburg, IL
Lawrence University, Appleton, WI
Lebanon Valley College, Annville, PA
Lees-McRae College, Banner Elk, NC
Lenoir Rhyne University, Hickory, NC
Luther College, Decorah, IA
Lycoming College, Williamsport, PA
Marietta College, Marietta, OH
Marshall University, Huntington, WV
McDaniel College, Westminster, MD
Mercer University, Macon, GA
Miami University, Oxford, OH
Moravian College, Bethlehem, PA
Muhlenberg College, Allentown, PA
Newberry College, Newberry, SC
Oglethorpe University, Atlanta, GA
Paul Smith's College, Paul Smiths, NY
Presbyterian College, Clinton, SC
Randolph-Macon College, Ashland, VA
Reed College, Portland, OR
Ripon College, Ripon, WI
Rollins College, Winter Park, FL
St. Francis College, Brooklyn Heights, NY
Samford University, Birmingham, AL
Stetson University, DeLand, FL
SUNY College at Cortland, Cortland, NY
Susquehanna University, Selinsgrove, PA
Thiel College, Greenville, PA
Tuskegee University, Tuskegee, AL
University of the South, Sewanee, TN

Virginia Wesleyan College, Norfolk, VA

Warren Wilson College, Asheville, NC

Washington and Lee University, Lexington, VA

West Virginia Wesleyan College, Buchanan, WV

Willamette University, Salem, OR

William Jewell College, Liberty, MO

Wittenberg University, Springfield, OH

Xavier University, Cincinnati, OH

## TUITION AND HOUSING

Tuition and fees at Duke were $31,500 in 2012–2013, but you'll need to add to that your living expenses, which are another $18,500, bringing the total to attend Duke to $50,000 a year. Note that graduate student housing is limited.

There are additional charges for health care and for having a car on campus.

Students entering Duke via the back gateway have the option for a flat-fee tuition plan, and you'll need to check with the master of environmental management and master of forestry program departments for details, since these can vary depending on academic and assistantship requirements.

## YET ANOTHER BACK GATEWAY

There is another little-known and rarely entered Duke back gateway. This one opens into the institution's prestigious Pratt School of Engineering via another 3/2 dual-degree program, albeit one with but a single cooperating institution: little Whitman College (enrollment 1,450), in Walla Walla, Washington.

The Whitman-Duke program leads to a bachelor of arts with a

major in natural and mathematical sciences from Whitman College *and* a bachelor of science with a major in computer science or a field of engineering from Duke University. The first three years of this five-year program are spent at Whitman, and the last two years at Duke, where the student is expected to complete courses in computer science or one of the branches of engineering.

For more information about the Nicholas School 3/2 program, contact:

Duke University
Office of Undergraduate Admissions
2138 Campus Drive
Box 90586
Durham, NC 27708
(919) 684-3214
Website: www.duke.edu

Nicholas School of the Environment
Box 90328 Duke University
Levine Science Research Center
Durham, NC 27708
(919) 613-8000
Website: www.env.duke.edu
Email: admissions@nicholas.duke.edu

For more information about the Whitman College-Pratt School of Engineering "Combined Plan," log on to the Whitman College website at www.whitman.edu/content/catalog/combined-plans.

# 15

## Engineering Genius: Caltech

---

■ **KEYBOX**

**SCHOOL:** California Institute of Technology (Caltech)

**LOCATION:** Pasadena, California

**COLLEGE RANKING:** 10

**GATE POSITION:** Ajar

**SAT REQUIRED:** No

**HOUSING:** Yes

**MINIMUM AGE:** 18

**APPLICATION CRITERIA:** High

**MEDIAN STARTING SALARY:** $69,700

**COST COMPARED TO FRONT GATEWAY:** Varies

---

Sarah was born and raised on the East Coast, where she excelled in math and science. Teachers started talking to her about applying to MIT in Boston, but Sarah had been thinking about Caltech, which she knew was ranked second internationally by *Times Higher Education World* in 2010 and first in the world among engineering and technology universities. Even more impressive, Caltech faculty members were cited in scholarly books and papers more often than any faculty anywhere else. This impressed her all the more because the school was actually quite small, with a total enrollment of 2,231 graduate and undergraduate students in 2012. And the Nobel Prize count among alumni and faculty was thirty-one and counting. Besides all this, Sarah was awfully curious to discover what it was like to live in a place without East Coast winters.

While Sarah was ready to take on the Caltech challenge (and, even with her grades and test scores, just getting in was hardly a sure thing) as well as the California sunshine, she was not ready for the $39,588 in annual tuition and fees and $12,084 room and board, which with living expenses came to more than $50,000. With the help of an advisor, she found a way to soften the blow. When the time came, she applied not directly to Caltech, but to Atlanta's Spelman College, one of thirteen institutions cooperating with the Pasadena school in a 3/2 dual-degree program.

## HOME OF THE FAMED PALOMAR OBSERVATORY

The world-class research and teaching institution that is Caltech began as a vocational school, Throop University, founded in 1891 by a local Pasadena businessman and political figure named Amos G. Throop. After being renamed twice over its first three decades—Throop Polytechnic Institute and Throop College of Technology—the school finally became California Institute of Technology in 1921.

By the 1910s, thanks largely to board member George Ellery Hale, a famed University of Chicago astronomer and the founder of the Mount Wilson Observatory, the institution was rapidly evolving into a prominent scientific university. America's entry into World War I in 1917 brought substantial funding for the development of advanced scientific and technological research at the institution, and the period between the world wars saw the rise of Caltech into truly national prominence. During the 1920s, a department of geology and a division of humanities and social sciences were established, along with a division of biology and a graduate school of aeronautics, which became the Jet Propulsion Laboratory and transformed Caltech into an international center for rocket science.

At the start of the 1930s, Caltech sponsored construction of the famed Palomar Observatory, completed eighteen years later, in 1948, with the installation of the two-hundred-inch Hale Telescope, which reigned as the largest optical telescope in the world for the next four decades. Also during the 1930s, an extraordinary visiting-scholars program was introduced, which brought the greatest minds in international physics to the Pasadena campus, including Paul Dirac, Erwin Schrödinger, Werner Heisenberg, Hendrik Lorentz, Niels Bohr, and Albert Einstein.

Throughout the twentieth century, Caltech faculty have been responsible for some of the most important milestones in modern science, including the discovery of antimatter; Linus Pauling's revolutionary work on the nature of the chemical bond in the 1930s; pioneering work in molecular biology through the 1960s; the foundation of modern earthquake science; work in creating nutritional standards; the discovery of quarks, the smallest building blocks of matter; early mapping of the human brain; advances in jet and rocket propulsion, flight, and control; and pioneering experimentation in the origin and nature of the universe.

## GETTING IN CAN BE DOWNRIGHT BRUTAL

Although Caltech calls sunny, prosperous Pasadena home, the learning experience at this university has been compared to a wilderness survival course for the mind. "We investigate the most challenging, fundamental problems in science and technology," the Caltech mission statement announces, and the institution's highly select faculty makes it their business to share the challenge with every student, graduate and undergraduate alike.

If the educational demands are rigorous in Caltech's science, math, and engineering programs, getting in can be downright brutal. For 2012, Caltech accepted just 12.6 percent of applicants.

They entered a program that offers twenty-four majors—called "options" by Caltech—and a half-dozen minors in six broad academic divisions: biology; chemistry and chemical engineering; engineering and applied science; geological and planetary sciences; humanities and social sciences; and physics, mathematics, and astronomy. In addition, interdisciplinary programs in applied physics, biochemistry, bioengineering, computation and neural systems, control and dynamical systems, environmental science and engineering, geobiology and astrobiology, geochemistry, and planetary astronomy are available. Most undergraduates major in mechanical engineering, physics, biology, chemical engineering, or computer and information sciences. Whatever "option" a student chooses, every Caltech undergrad must follow a core curriculum that includes five terms of mathematics, five of physics, two of chemistry, one of biology, a freshman elective, two terms of lab courses, two of science writing, and a full twelve terms in the humanities. Caltech wants its engineers and scientists grounded in a full liberal education.

## CALTECH'S BACK GATEWAY

You can enter the back gateway to Caltech through a 3/2 dual-degree program jointly administered with a baker's dozen of cooperating colleges across the country. After three years at one of the cooperating institutions and two years at Caltech, you receive a dual degree. Currently, the participating institutions are:

Bowdoin College, Brunswick, ME
Bryn Mawr College, Bryn Mawr, PA
Grinnell College, Grinnell, IA
Haverford College, Haverford, PA
Mount Holyoke College, South Hadley, MA
Oberlin College, Oberlin, OH

Occidental College, Los Angeles, CA
Ohio Wesleyan, Delaware, OH
Pomona College, Claremont, CA
Reed College, Portland, OR
Spelman College, Atlanta, GA
Wesleyan University, Middletown, CT
Whitman College, Walla Walla, WA

Enrolling in one of the participating colleges and surviving three years there by no means guarantees you admission to the 3/2 program. Whether or not you get in is wholly determined by the Caltech Upperclass Admissions Committee, which looks for applicants who have amassed "a record of superior academic achievement at their home institutions, and [who have earned] strong letters of recommendation from their 3/2 liaison and from a mathematics, science, or engineering faculty member." During the three years spent at the participating college, you must have completed a minimum of one year of physics and one year of mathematics, including multivariable calculus and differential equations, as well as one year of chemistry. These, however, are *minimum* requirements. The committee strongly recommends *two* years of mathematics and physics.

Caltech expects the participating colleges to determine which of the Caltech "options" (majors) are appropriate for their students. This means that some participating colleges may choose to limit a potential 3/2 program transferee to opting for an engineering major or some other field not typically available at liberal arts colleges.

## How to Apply

Detailed application instructions are available at the Caltech website. Log on to www.admissions.caltech.edu; after reading the material there, you can download the required admissions form, together with instructions, at www.admissions.caltech.edu/applying/forms. All application forms and supporting material, including the all-important letters of recommendation from your home college's Caltech liaison and from a faculty member in math, science, or engineering, are due at Caltech by April 1.

While 3/2 transfer applicants are not required to submit SAT or ACT scores, they must take entrance examinations in mathematics and physics, which are given after submission of a transfer application. Students must find a proctor at their home institution to administer the required four-hour math exam and the three-hour physics exam. Caltech admissions officers advise applicants to prepare themselves in the following areas of physics:

| | |
|---|---|
| Newtonian mechanics | Ellipses |
| Work and energy | Electric fields and potentials |
| Energy conservation | Gauss's Law |
| Momentum | Current resistance |
| Rigid rotations | Capacitance |
| Angular momentum | Inductance |
| Harmonic motion | Magnetic fields |
| Resonance | Faraday's law |
| Gravity | AC/DC circuits |
| Kepler orbits | Special relativity |

In math, they advise pre-exam preparation in:

| | |
|---|---|
| Basic calculus | Vectors and matrices |
| Taylor polynomials | Determinants |
| Series | Vector spaces |
| Linear algebra | Transformation |
| Systems of equations | Vector calculus |

## Typical 3/2 Scenarios

Requirements and procedures vary from one participating institution to another, but consider the following two examples as typical.

Students who choose the dual-degree path at Spelman College, for example, are asked to declare a major in engineering, physics, chemistry, computer science, or math and complete the requirements for the major. At least six months before their intended transfer to Caltech, they must register with the dual-degree office at Spelman.

This historically black women's college, located west of downtown Atlanta, Georgia, was started in a church basement in 1881 to teach former slaves to read and write. An endowment from oil tycoon and philanthropist John D. Rockefeller enabled Spelman to transform itself into a modern college, and a $20 million gift from entertainer Bill Cosby and his wife Camille, whose two daughters attended Spelman, has provided extraordinary resources.

Spelman's acceptance rate was 37.6 percent in 2012–2013 (compared with 12.8 percent for those who apply directly to Caltech). Most students, roughly 80 percent, come from out of state. Applications for regular admission are due February 1, at a cost of $35 for those who apply by mail and $25 online. Besides the usual standardized test scores, high school transcripts, and two recommendations, applicants are required to write a personal essay discussing their commitment to knowledge and service.

Another institution that participates in Caltech's dual-degree program is Occidental College, also a small college in a big city—in this case, Los Angeles. Occidental approaches the 3/2 "combined plan" in a way that offers students considerable latitude in their choice of an eventual Caltech major. The overall objective of the Occidental approach is to prepare students for entrance into an outstanding engineering school by giving them the strongest possible liberal arts foundation. To qualify for application to Caltech from Occidental, a recommendation by the liaison officer is required, in addition to a minimum B+ grade average in science and math and a grade average of B or higher in other courses.

The acceptance rate at Occidental was 41.9 percent in 2011–2012. With 2,089 full-time students enrolled, the student-faculty ratio is 10 to 1. The admission deadline is January 10, and the fee is $50. Occidental accepts the Common Application, but it also requires a personal essay that addresses one of three questions:

What inspires genuine passion in your life?
What person or character best represents your generation?
What is the one important question that you wish we had asked?

Both Spelman and Occidental have significantly higher acceptance rates than Caltech. Spelman is also an example of an institution that is more affordable, with tuition and fees at $23,794 and room and board $11.541 for 2012–2013. Costs at Occidental, however, were even higher than those at Caltech for 2012–2013: $44,570 tuition and $12,450 room and board. The lesson here is that, for some, the 3/2 program will not only better their odds of getting into Caltech, it will also reduce the cost of the degree, even though it adds a year, since students pay the going rate at the participating college for three years followed by Caltech tuition for two years. But take notice: Some participating colleges have "most selective" acceptance policies that are comparable to those at Caltech, and some are equally (or even more!) expensive to attend. If you are looking to a 3/2 program to provide a back gateway, be certain to do your research and plan well ahead.

## TUITION AND HOUSING

Once you get to Caltech, fees can vary, depending on campus living at a single, double, or quad apartment or if you opt for off-campus living.

Any way you look at it, expect to pay close to $70,000 a year. Tuition plus mandatory fees alone total $40,000. Your cost of living on this quiet, residential campus in Pasadena, eleven miles northeast from Los Angeles, will range from $21,000 to almost $30,000, depending on the accommodations you choose. And remember that these are only estimates for 2012–2013 and are based on a single graduate student's expenses.

For more information, contact:

California Institute of Technology
Office of Undergraduate Admissions
1200 E. California Boulevard
Pasadena, CA 91125
(626) 395-6341
Website: www.caltech.edu
Email: ugadmissions@caltech.edu

# 16

## Elite Bargain:
## Northwestern University

---

**■ KEYBOX**

SCHOOL: Northwestern University

LOCATION: Evanston, Illinois

COLLEGE RANKING: 12

GATE POSITION: Wide open

SAT REQUIRED: No

HOUSING: None

MINIMUM AGE: 18

APPLICATION CRITERIA: Moderate

MEDIAN STARTING SALARY: $49,800

COST COMPARED TO FRONT GATEWAY: Half

---

When he was just sixteen, Ed dropped out of high school to work on the family's Midwestern farm. It was not something he had planned or wanted to do, but his dad had been badly injured in a fall off a combine, and there was no one else who could take over the daily operations of the farm. It was up to Ed to keep the family business—and the family—afloat.

After a long convalescence, Ed's father recovered sufficiently to resume his farm work part-time, which gave Ed just the opportunity he needed to study for, take, and pass the General Educational Development (GED) exam. As his father's health continued to improve, Ed even found the time to earn an associate of arts (A.A.) degree at the nearby community college. There, his English professor told him about his own beloved alma mater, Northwestern University, which was not so far away, in the stately Chicago suburb of Evanston, Illinois.

It was, his professor explained, not an easy school to get into, and he had the stats to prove it. Taking out the latest edition of *U.S. News & World Report's Best Colleges*, he showed Ed that, for 2012, 18 percent of applicants were accepted. More than 90 percent of these were in the top tenth of their high school class. Nor was this elite private university cheap. For 2012–2013, tuition and fees were $43,779, with room and board adding an additional $13,329. But, Ed's professor continued, there was a back gateway—and he thought it was perfect for somebody like Ed.

## BORDERING CHICAGO ON
## THE LAKE MICHIGAN SHORE

Among many, Northwestern University has long enjoyed a reputation as the most elite private college in the Midwest. Located in Evanston, a sophisticated town bordering Chicago on the shore of Lake Michigan, the university offers the kind of tranquil campus experience typically associated with the Ivy League while also allowing students to partake in the vibrant urban life and culture of one of the nation's great cities.

Northwestern's original 240-acre campus in Evanston is home to the College of Arts and Sciences, the Graduate School, and the Business School. Primly arrayed between the lakeshore and the town, the North Campus in Evanston is also home to the fraternity quads, the Henry Crown Sports Pavilion and other athletic facilities, the Technological Institute, Dearborn Observatory, and other science-related buildings. From the South Campus, also part of the Evanston facility, rise the humanities buildings, music buildings, and art buildings, including the splendid Mary and Leigh Block Museum of Art. South campus is also home to the sorority quads. Like many other businesses and institutions in the Chicago area, Northwestern University expanded eastward with a lake fill, adding eighty-four acres of campus in the 1960s. This area houses the 4.6 million–volume University Library, the Norris University Center (the student union), and the Pick-Staiger Concert Hall.

Although "Northwestern" may seem a nondescript geographical name for a university, it is actually of great historical significance. On May 31, 1850, nine of Chicago's leading businessmen resolved to found a university to serve what had been, just a half century earlier, the Northwest Territory of the United States: the nation's frontier and gateway to the vast West. From the beginning, therefore, the school proclaimed its identification with the expanding heartland of America. Indeed, when the Illinois General Assembly granted a charter to the "Trustees of the North Western University" on January 28, 1851, the institution became the very first chartered university in Illinois.

During the 1870s and 1880s Northwestern extended its reach into the professional realm by affiliating with existing schools of law, medicine, and dentistry based in Chicago. Within a short time, the reputation and wealth of the Evanston-based institution motivated these affiliate schools to fully integrate themselves with Northwestern. By the end of the nineteenth century, therefore, Northwestern was recognized as a major research university; however, it was not until 1920 that construction of the Chicago campus, designed by architect James Gamble Rogers, began, with the purpose of housing professional schools. During the period of construction, from 1920 to 1939, there was much talk of merging Northwestern with the city's Southside educational powerhouse, the University of Chicago (today rated by *U.S. News & World Report* fourth among U.S. colleges), but that scheme never went forward.

## EXCEPTIONAL UNDERGRADS

Described by *U.S. News & World Report* as "most selective," Northwestern attracts exceptional undergraduates. Somewhat more than half of those accepted enroll in arts and sciences at the Judd A. and Marjorie Weinberg College of Arts and Sciences, and the rest choose to study in one of five professional schools:

- School of Communication
- Henry and Leigh Bienen School of Music
- Robert R. McCormick School of Engineering and Applied Science
- Medill School of Journalism
- School of Education and Social Policy

Like the Weinberg College, the professional schools all enjoy national reputations, but the McCormick School of Engineering and Applied Science and the Medill School of Journalism are particular standouts.

## THE BACK GATEWAY

South of Evanston, in the lakefront Streeterville neighborhood near Chicago's downtown Loop district, is the university's twenty-five-acre Chicago Campus. It is home to an internationally renowned medical school and hospital, a distinguished law school, a part-time business school, and the School of Continuing Studies (SCS), which has long offered evening and weekend courses for working adults and is also the back gateway to the university. Students attending SCS may take classes either at the Chicago or Evanston campus. (Late in 2008,

Northwestern added a third campus—far from both Evanston and Chicago, in Education City, Doha, Qatar.) The mission of Northwestern's School of Continuing Studies (SCS) "is to be the lifelong partner of adult learners who seek a superior educational experience at Northwestern University." There is, in other words, no difference between an undergraduate degree earned through SCS and one earned at any of the other Northwestern schools open to undergraduates.

SCS offers hundreds of courses in more than thirty subjects and sixteen bachelor degree majors. You may work toward one of three degrees: the bachelor of philosophy (B.Phil.) or bachelor of science in general studies (B.S.G.S.) degree conferred by the Judd A. and Marjorie Weinberg College of Arts and Sciences, the largest college at Northwestern, or the bachelor of philosophy in communication (B. Phil.Com.) degree from the School of Communication. You may major in any of the following:

Anthropology (B.Phil. or B.S.G.S.)
Art history (B.Phil. or B.S.G.S.)
Biological sciences: human biology (B.Phil. or B.S.G.S.)
Communication studies (B.Phil.Com.)
Communication systems (B.Phil.Com.)
Economics (B.Phil. or B.S.G.S.)
English and American literature (B.Phil. or B.S.G.S.)
English major in writing (B.Phil. or B.S.G.S.)
History (B.Phil. or B.S.G.S.)
Information systems (B.Phil. or B.S.G.S.)
Mathematics (B.Phil. or B.S.G.S.)
Organization behavior (B.Phil. or B.S.G.S.)
Political science (B.Phil. or B.S.G.S.)
Psychology (B.Phil. or B.S.G.S.)
Radio/TV/film (B.Phil.Com.)
Sociology (B.Phil. or B.S.G.S.)

Additionally, you may combine any of these majors with a minor in:

| | |
|---|---|
| Anthropology | Information systems |
| Art history | Journalism |
| Biological sciences | Mathematics |
| Business | Organization behavior |
| Economics | Political science |
| English: minor in literature | Psychology |
| English: minor in writing | Sociology |
| History | |

Northwestern began offering continuing education, in the form of evening liberal arts classes, back in 1905. Beginning in 1908, the very year it opened its doors, the School of Commerce (now the Kellogg School of Management) offered business evening courses. The Medill School of Journalism began its evening program in 1921. In 1933, University College was created primarily for adult education and other part-time learning. In 1954, University College merged with the evening undergraduate program of the School of Commerce, and in 1983 the merged programs became part of a wider Division of Continuing Education. This was renamed the School of Continuing Studies in 2000.

Although SCS is designed primarily to serve the needs of adult learners, the minimum age for admission is eighteen. As with the rest of Northwestern University, SCS courses are offered on a quarterly calendar.

## TUITION AND HOUSING

For 2012, SCS tuition was $1,495 per credit hour, a little less than half the per-unit cost for traditional, front gateway Northwestern students, making this an extraordinary value in higher education.

Although on-campus housing is not available to SCS students,

Northwestern's Off-Campus Housing Office (www.northwestern.edu/living/options/off-campus.html) provides listings of nearby rooms, apartments, and houses for rent. Because housing near both the Evanston and Chicago campuses is in high demand, you should make your housing arrangements well before arriving on campus.

## How to Apply

Admission requirements for SCS are considerably less rigorous than those at other colleges in the university; nevertheless, you do have some work to do. Begin by completing and submitting the SCS Application for Undergraduate Admission online at https://nu.askadmissions.net/emtinterestpage.aspx?ip=app. There is no paper application. Deadlines are August 1 for the fall quarter; November 1 for winter; February 1 for spring; and May 1 for summer. The Admissions Committee accepts applications year-round, and you can expect to be notified of your admission status about three weeks after you submit your *complete* application. This consists of:

- The online application, including personal statement
- A nonrefundable $50 application fee
- An official high school transcript (or GED report)
- Official transcripts from all previously attended colleges and universities
- Documentation of English proficiency, if your first language is not English

Among other things, the online application requires submitting your educational history, and the Admissions Committee strongly recommends that you include a full résumé as well, showing any work experience. You will be asked to specify which degree program you are seeking to enter and your intended major. The required personal statement is a "5,000-character" essay that explains how the degree program will help you meet your academic and career goals. Expect to be asked to respond to the following statement: "Describe your academic and personal goals and how these will be furthered by study at SCS. Feel free to include information related to your major course of study, previous academic work and professional aspirations." You do not have to submit SAT or ACT scores.

The Admissions Committee recommends that, as a degree-seeking applicant, you apply for a performance-based admission. This will give you an opportunity to prove yourself by actual course work. The committee will make a provisional admission decision, with your ultimate admission status depending on your performance in four courses completed after submission of the application. The minimum performance threshold for full admission to a degree program is a B average in the initial four courses.

For more information, contact:

Northwestern University
School of Continuing Studies
Undergraduate Admissions
405 Church Street
Evanston, IL 60208
(847) 491-5611
Website: scs@northwestern.edu
Email: scsadmissions@northwestern.edu

Northwestern University
SCS Admissions
339 East Chicago Avenue
Wieboldt Hall, Sixth Floor
Chicago, Illinois 60611

(312) 503-0875
Email: scsadmissions@northwestern.edu


For off-campus housing help, contact:

Off-Campus Housing Office
Engelhart Hall
1915 Maple Avenue
Evanston, Illinois 60201
(847) 491-5127
Website: www.northwestern.edu/living/options/off-campus.html

# 17

## Public Ivy:
## The University of Virginia

---

**▓ KEYBOX**

SCHOOL: University of Virginia

LOCATION: Charlottesville, Virginia

COLLEGE RANKING: 24

GATE POSITION: Half-open to wide open, depending on
      program

SAT REQUIRED: No

HOUSING: Available, depending on program

MINIMUM AGE: 20

APPLICATION CRITERIA: Moderate

MEDIAN STARTING SALARY: $52,200

COST COMPARED TO FRONT GATEWAY: Same or significantly less,
      depending on program

---

Claire's parents had always hoped she would choose a career in law
or medicine, but they were concerned that her high school grades,
though good enough to put her in the upper quarter of her class, fell
short of the top 10 percent. This didn't much bother Claire, whose academic goal, she believed, was less demanding than pre-med or pre-law.
She just wanted to study American history, especially the colonial
period. This didn't mean she hadn't set her sights on a particular school.

For her, the magnet was the University of Virginia (UVA), the school founded by none other than Thomas Jefferson.

When the time came, Claire applied to her dream school. What she had not bothered to consider, however, was that about 90 percent of those accepted to UVA are in the top tenth of their high school graduating class. For the 2012–2013 academic year, Claire's application was not one of the 33.3 percent accepted. Claire was down, but far from out. While she could not rewrite her own academic history, she did find a back gateway into Mr. Jefferson's university.

## FATHERED BY THOMAS JEFFERSON

Thomas Jefferson, who died on July 4, 1826, is buried in a hillside family plot at Monticello, the home he designed and built in the Blue Ridge foothills. An obelisk (also his own design) bears the inscription he himself composed for it:

*Here was buried*
*Thomas Jefferson*
*Author of the Declaration of American Independence*
*of the Statute of Virginia for religious freedom*
*and Father of the University of Virginia*

The epitaph is less remarkable for the profound résumé items it includes than for what it leaves out. It seems that the nation's third chief executive thought that "fathering" the University of Virginia in 1819 had been a greater achievement than serving as the American president who (among other things) acquired the vast Louisiana Territory.

As Jefferson saw it, education was the key to maintaining and improving a democratic nation. Not only was he the prime mover behind UVA, he was its first architect—the neoclassical design of the main campus and the oldest buildings on that campus are his work—as well as the designer of its first curriculum. What is more, he ensured that the university was built not on the established Eastern Seaboard with its old, aristocratic wealth, but farther west, in Charlottesville, amid the rolling piedmont of the Blue Ridge Mountains, not far from Monticello, a site on the forward-looking cusp of the national frontier. He proclaimed that the university would be dedicated to the "illimitable freedom of the human mind" and that faculty and students would be encouraged to "follow truth wherever it might lead."

Ever since its founding in 1819, UVA has attracted some of the country's best and brightest, making it a rarity among Southern state universities—an institution of genuine national, not just regional, renown. As *U.S. News & World Report* put it, this state school is "chock full of academic stars who turn down private schools like Duke, Princeton and Cornell" for what they consider a better bargain academically and financially.

The list of distinguished UVA alumni is long and varied, ranging from Edgar Allan Poe and Georgia O'Keeffe to President Woodrow Wilson, Robert F. Kennedy (as well as his son Robert F. Kennedy Jr.), and Senator Edward Kennedy. Polar explorer Admiral Richard Byrd graduated from the university, as did no fewer than five NASA astronauts.

UVA is first among state-supported universities in the number of Rhodes Scholars it has produced—forty-six as of 2009. *U.S. News & World Report* ranks the school the twenty-fourth best university in the nation, and it deservedly remains one of the eight state schools author Richard Moll (in his 1985 *Public Ivies: A Guide to America's Best Public Undergraduate Colleges and Universities*) classified as a "public ivy."

UVA's $5.24 billion endowment is the largest per capita of any public university. Enrolling 15,762 full-time undergraduate students for 2012–2013, UVA offers fifty-one bachelor's degrees in forty-seven fields. Its vast library system holds five million volumes in addition to the resources of its Electronic Text Center, which affords access to more digitized texts than any other university in the world.

Undergraduate student life is rich. Student and faculty art is exhibited in the gallery of the McIntire Department of Art, while the University of Virginia Art Museum features both permanent and traveling international collections from ancient times to the present day. The Department of Drama produces theater and dance events—six plays and musicals and two dance concerts yearly, in addition to performances by many guest artists—and the department also sponsors the Heritage Theatre Festival, which attracts audiences from the entire region. The McIntire Department of Music sponsors many faculty- and student-directed ensembles in all musical styles.

Virginia has long been a force in collegiate athletics. The men's and women's swimming, women's rowing, and men's and women's lacrosse teams are what the *Fiske Guide to Colleges* calls "perennial powerhouses." There are also sixteen intramural sports leagues in everything from flag football to inner-tube water polo, and sixty-three club sports organizations. *Newsweek* recently named UVA "Hottest for Fitness" because 94 percent of the students regularly use four state-of-the-art indoor athletic facilities.

As for the university's hometown, Charlottesville, it may have been relatively remote in the days of Thomas Jefferson, but today it is just 120 miles from the historical, commercial, and cultural attractions of Washington, DC.

## UVA'S BACK GATEWAYS

There are actually two back gateways to the University of Virginia, the first of which comes with something rare in the realm of college admissions: a guarantee. Since 2006, any student who attends a community college in Virginia and completes a set of specified requirements is guaranteed admission to the UVA College of Arts and Sciences. In fact, during recent years, students from Virginia's community colleges have made up a full third of all UVA transfers. You will find detailed requirements for transferring from Virginia community colleges to UVA at the university website (www.admission.virginia.edu/vccsguide), but here are the principal requirements:

- You must be at least twenty years old.
- You must have completed an associate in arts, associate in science, or associate in arts and science degree from a community college in the state of Virginia.
- You must have earned a minimum of fifty-four transferable credit hours, with a minimum of forty-five of those earned within the Virginia Community College System (VCCS).
- You must have a minimum 3.4 grade point average, with a C grade or higher in every VCCS course taken, except for specified English courses, in which you must have earned a grade of B or higher.

Once admitted as a transfer student from a Virginia community college, you will have to meet specific requirements for completion of your degree. These include:

- Maintaining full-time enrollment with a course load of 15 credits each semester
- Declaring a major by the end of the first UVA semester
- Earning a total of 120 credits, with a minimum of 60 at UVA
- Completing all course work, major requirements, and graduation requirements within four semesters

The second back gateway to UVA does not come with a guarantee, it offers only one degree—a bachelor of interdisciplinary studies (B.I.S.)—and it is specifically geared to the needs of part-time, adult learners. The B.I.S. program was established in 2001 by the School of Continuing and Professional Studies. The degree program consists of part-time study in evening classes, which are offered year-round on the Charlottesville campus as well as at Tidewater Community College (four campuses, in Chesapeake, Norfolk, Portsmouth/Suffolk, and Virginia Beach) and Northern Virginia Community College (Alexandria, Annandale, Loudoun, Manassas, and Woodbridge). The B.I.S. curriculum provides a broadly based liberal studies education that offers specific concentrations in business, humanities, social sciences, or education (the latter leading to teacher certification).

While standardized exams such as the SAT are not required for admission, you must satisfy the following requirements:

- You must have graduated from high school at least four years prior to enrolling.
- You must have completed sixty hours of *transferable* college-level work with a grade of 2.0 or better from one or more regionally accredited colleges or universities, including any required prerequisites for your chosen concentration. ("Transferable" courses are those normally eligible for transfer to UVA; for details, go to http://saz-webdmz.eservices.virginia.edu/asequivs.)
- Within your sixty transferable hours, thirty must satisfy the requirements of the UVA Liberal Studies Core. This generally translates to six credit hours of English composition; six credit hours of humanities; six credit hours of social sciences; and twelve credit hours of mathematics and/or natural science. For additional details, go to http://records.ureg.virginia.edu/index.php.
- You must have a minimum cumulative grade point average (GPA) of 2.0 from the institution you most recently attended.
- You must be in good financial standing at UVA.

There is no formal computer competency requirement, but you will be assumed to possess basic computer proficiency.

Classes meet at night except during the summer, when they are offered at night or on weekends. You are required to take a minimum of one class per term, but if you have the time and scheduling flexibility, you may choose (with an advisor's approval) to carry a full-time course load of twelve to fifteen credits. You may also be granted permission to enroll in courses in another school of the university after consultation with and approval of B.I.S. staff.

B.I.S. students can expect to tackle topics from a cross-disciplinary perspective, with special emphasis on critical thinking and analysis. The curriculum includes liberal studies seminars, a chosen concentration, a selection of elective courses, and what is called a "capstone" research project, which you choose in consultation with faculty members. You will select your electives from the regular undergraduate offerings of the schools of Arts and Sciences, Commerce, and Engineering.

## How to Apply

To apply to the *first* UVA back gateway—transferring to the UVA School of Arts and Sciences from a Virginia community college—first make certain that you have completed the requirements, then obtain an application form from the Office of Admission, University of Virginia, P.O. Box 400160, Charlottesville, Virginia 22904. Complete the application and ensure that you mail it in good time to arrive at the Office of Admission no later than March 1 for the fall term.

To apply for the *second* back gateway—enrollment in the B.I.S. program at the School of Continuing and Professional Studies—complete the following steps:

1. Make an appointment with a B.I.S. admissions advisor by calling (434) 982-5274 or emailing buzzoni@virginia.edu.
2. Obtain an application form from the B.I.S. office.
3. Complete the application, including the Application for Virginia In-State Education Privileges if you are seeking in-state tuition eligibility.
4. Provide official transcripts from all previously attended colleges or universities. These transcripts may be sent directly to the B.I.S. office: Bachelor of Interdisciplinary Studies, UVA School

of Continuing and Professional Studies, P.O. Box 400764, Charlottesville, VA 22904-4764.

5. Pay the $60 application fee.
6. If English is not your native language, provide TOEFL (Test of English as a Foreign Language) scores.

Note that the fall deadline for submission of the completed application is July 1, and the spring deadline is November 15.

All those accepted into the B.I.S. program, which totaled about two hundred students in 2010, are admitted on a provisional basis. You will have four consecutive terms after admission in which to successfully complete a computer competency requirement, two liberal studies seminars, two other B.I.S. courses, and any prerequisites or credit hour requirements that were not satisfied at the time of admission. You will be expected to maintain at least a 2.0 average in your course work. Achieve all of this, and your provisional status converts to full admission to the degree program.

## TUITION AND HOUSING

For students who are transferring to the College of Arts and Sciences from a Virginia community college, tuition and fees are identical to those paid by front gateway students. In-state tuition and fees were $12,006 for 2012–2013 (plus $9,419 for room and board). Out-of-state tuition and fees were $38,018 (plus $9,419 for room and board).

For B.I.S. students, in-state tuition (2012–2013 academic year) was $343 per credit hour, plus a required fee of $207 per term. Out-of-state tuition jumped to $1,085 per credit hour, plus a required fee of $266 per term. These costs amount to about one-third of the cost of tuition paid by front gateway students, and financial aid, including scholarships, is available. Log on to www.scps.virginia.edu/bisdegree/tuition.php for the latest information.

Students enrolled in the College of Arts and Sciences as transferees from Virginia community colleges are eligible for on-campus housing, but B.I.S. students are not eligible. The school does, however, offer resources to help you find suitable off-campus rooms, apartments, and houses.

For more information about transferring to the College of Arts and Sciences from a Virginia community college, contact:

Office of Undergraduate Admissions
P.O. Box 400160
University of Virginia
Charlottesville, VA 22904
(434) 982-3200
Fax: (434) 924-3587
Website: www.admission.virginia.edu/vccsguide
Email: undergradadmission@virginia.edu

For more information about enrolling in the B.I.S. program at the School of Continuing and Professional Studies, contact:

Bachelor of Interdisciplinary Studies Staff
University of Virginia
School of Continuing and Professional Studies
106 Midmont Lane
P.O. Box 400764
Charlottesville, VA 22904
(434) 243-5086
Website: www.scps.virginia.edu/bisdegree
Email: klb7r@virginia.edu

# 18

## Liberal Studies at Georgetown University

> **■ KEYBOX**
>
> SCHOOL: Georgetown University
>
> LOCATION: Washington, DC
>
> COLLEGE RANKING: 21
>
> GATE POSITION: Wide open
>
> SAT REQUIRED: No
>
> HOUSING: Limited
>
> MINIMUM AGE: 18
>
> APPLICATION CRITERIA: Moderate
>
> MEDIAN STARTING SALARY: $57,000
>
> COST COMPARED TO FRONT GATEWAY: About half

The reddish-brown Romanesque buildings of Georgetown University tower over the banks of the Potomac River and overlook the nation's capital. Georgetown is the oldest Catholic university in the United States, founded in 1789, the very year the authors of the Constitution signed their work. The school came of age with the nation, and today it is especially renowned as an academic center for public policy, global business, and international relations. Georgetown has long represented academic entrée into the corridors of national power as well as a portal to the cultural riches of Washington, DC. Celebrated alumni include six serving U.S. senators, sixteen members of the House of Representatives, former secretary of defense Robert Gates, and the outgoing national security advisor General James L. Jones. Associate Supreme Court Justice Antonin Scalia is a graduate, as are many U.S. diplomats and a dozen serving or former international heads of state, including President Bill Clinton.

Rated twenty-first among U.S. colleges overall by *U.S. News & World Report* in *Best Colleges 2013*, Georgetown is—no surprise—among the "most selective" of American universities. In 2012, 18.1 percent of applicants were accepted. Nor does the Georgetown experience come cheap. For 2012–2013, tuition and fees were $42,870 and room and board $13,632. Fortunately, there is a back gateway for those barred by a less than stellar academic record or a less than bulging wallet.

## COMMITTED TO A RIGOROUS EDUCATION

Georgetown is a Jesuit university, and it takes seriously what it calls its "Jesuit and Catholic identity," demonstrating a commitment not only to rigorous education (a Jesuit hallmark for nearly five centuries) but also to faith. About half of the school's undergraduates are Catholic, but religion is never used as a criterion for admission, and all major faiths are practiced and encouraged on campus. In addition to on-campus Catholic clergy, including many professors, Georgetown employs a Buddhist and a rabbi to counsel students of those faiths, and it was the first American university to employ a full-time Muslim imam on campus. In any given week, according to university officials, more than fifty different religious services take place across the Georgetown campus, including Roman Catholic Masses, Muslim prayer services, Orthodox Christian services, Jewish Shabbat services, Protestant services, and Bible studies.

There was, of course, no District of Columbia in 1634 when English

Jesuits founded Maryland as a haven for Roman Catholics in the predominantly Protestant colonies of British North America. Although the Jesuits established a number of schools in the colony prior to the American Revolution, it was not until 1789 that John Carroll, archbishop of Maryland and head of the Roman Catholic Church in the United States, acquired the first sixty acres of the property on which Georgetown College would be built.

Classes commenced in 1792, and Georgetown awarded its first two bachelor's degrees in 1817. At the approach of the Civil War in 1859, the Georgetown student body numbered 313, but it fell precipitously to a mere seventeen after the outbreak of the war in 1861. Some campus buildings were pressed into wartime service as hospitals. After the war ended in 1865, the school rapidly recovered and began to make academic, social, and political history as Father Patrick F. Healy, S.J., became not only the first African American to earn a Ph.D., but also the first to lead a major American university, serving as Georgetown's president from 1873 to 1882. Healy transformed the institution by emphasizing and cultivating the departments of history and the natural sciences, and he left his imprint on the look of the campus by building in 1877 the distinctive Flemish Romanesque structure today called Healy Hall.

From the 1980s onward, Georgetown University not only continued to grow, but became increasingly diverse, and in 2001 John J. DeGioia, Ph.D., was named the university's first lay president. Today the university employs more than five thousand faculty and staff and enrolls more than seven thousand undergraduates and eight thousand graduate students.

There are eight schools within the university:

- Georgetown College, the oldest and largest of the university's school, is the principal undergraduate college.
- McDonough School of Business, founded in 1957, offers both undergraduate and graduate degrees in business.

- Edmund A. Walsh School of Foreign Service has been open to undergraduate and graduate students since 1919, and also offers professional diplomats a variety of "midcareer programs."
- Georgetown Law is one of the nation's most respected law schools, which confers a law degree and also offers programs of continuing legal education. The school boasts the fifth largest law library in the nation.
- The Graduate School of Arts and Sciences offers graduate programs in thirty-four departments.
- The School of Medicine, like the School of Law, is a top-tier choice for those seeking a professional degree.
- The School of Nursing and Health Studies is open to undergraduate as well as graduate students and additionally offers second-degree programs.
- The School of Continuing Studies (SCS) is geared to meet the needs of "professionals, students and life-long learners [who want] to improve themselves and improve the world around them." SCS also serves as Georgetown University's back gateway, via its bachelor of liberal studies (B.A.L.S.) degree program.

Representing as they do more than a hundred different nations, Georgetown undergraduates surely make up one of the most diverse student bodies in the United States. Nevertheless, they tend to share certain values. About half are Catholic, but an even greater number are committed to an ethic of service, either charitable or governmental, and are well known for political activism and volunteerism. They are also willing to embrace the demanding Jesuit spirit of uncompromising education. The school's broad but traditional liberal arts curriculum fosters intellectual prowess and moral rigor in students. Every student must satisfy requirements in humanities, writing, philosophy, and theology. Beyond this, the four schools open to undergraduates have their own requirements. All, however, partake in a similar strong multidisciplinary and intercultural orientation. A total of 38 percent of students study abroad through university-sponsored programs in ninety countries.

## GEORGETOWN'S BACK GATEWAY

Established more than a half century ago, the School of Continuing Studies (SCS) today offers "a wide range of educational options to a diverse community of students and professionals" with more than 665 credit and noncredit courses. About three thousand students attend SCS each year. Eight graduate-level degree and certification programs and one undergraduate degree, the bachelor of arts in liberal studies (B.A.L.S.), are offered.

As with continuing education programs at other major universities, SCS was primarily designed for working adults, with classes scheduled in the evenings and on Saturdays. "You can complete your entire degree," officials promise, "without ever setting foot in a classroom during traditional working hours." Thirteen programs—called "concentrations"—lead to the B.A.L.S. degree:

American studies
Catholic studies
Classical civilizations
Communications
Ethics and the professions
Humanities
International affairs
Leadership
Literature and society
Religious studies
Social and public policy

The theory and practice of American democracy
Urban analysis and community development

As an alternative to these prescribed concentrations you may select an "Individualized Study" option and work with faculty to create your own custom area of concentration.

The B.A.L.S. degree requires forty-eight credits (sixteen three-credit courses) in your concentration; however, you may choose to write a thesis in your concentration, which will count toward a certain number of required credits. There is little pressure to declare a concentration quickly. You may do so at any time, and you may change your concentration at any time.

Whatever concentration you choose, you will be required to earn a total of 120 credits overall, including any transfer credits you may have, with a minimum GPA of 2.0. All degree candidates must take thirteen required core courses, which are designed to "provide the foundations for successful undergraduate study from the liberal studies perspective." Most of the core curriculum is intended to "acquaint you with the evolution of Western civilization from ancient times to the third millennium." The courses include:

Introduction to Ethics
Introduction to the Social Sciences
Greeks and Romans
Biblical Literature and the Ancient World
Medieval Thought and Culture
Faith and Reason in the Middle Ages
The Renaissance
The Early Modern World
Enlightenment, Revolution and Democracy
The Nineteenth Century
War and Peace

The New Millennium
Writing in an Interdisciplinary Environment

Finally, in addition to completing the concentration and core requirements, you must earn twenty-one credits (seven three-credit courses) in elective courses, which are defined as courses outside of your concentration.

Students may be admitted to liberal studies at the entry level or may be accepted as transfers from other institutions. About sixty approved transfer credits may generally be applied toward the B.A.L.S. degree. Moreover, with the approval of the associate dean, you may take for degree credit:

- A "limited number" of courses from units of Georgetown University outside of SCS
- A "limited number" of courses at other educational institutions in Washington, DC
- An independent study project, which you design with any willing Georgetown faculty member

Full details on the B.A.L.S. program are available online at http://scs .georgetown.edu/departments/4/bachelor-of-arts-in-liberal-studies/ about-the-program/curriculum#curriculum.

## How to Apply

Although SCS is specifically tailored to meet the needs of adult learners, the minimum age for admission is eighteen, and you can study part-time or full-time.

Neither SAT nor ACT scores are required for admission, and the academic requirements are far less stringent than those for traditional front gateway admission. You *will* need to have earned a minimum 2.0 GPA in your high school course work, but admissions officials encourage students who have been out of school for "a significant period of time" or who feel their grades do not "accurately reflect their academic ability" to submit supplementary information about their experiences that "relate directly to the proposed program of study."

SCS is thoroughly committed to helping students succeed. There are courses as well as individualized mentoring to help you bring your writing, logical, and rhetorical skills up to speed, and you will find a cadre of dedicated SCS academic advisors and faculty mentors on hand to provide one-on-one counseling and support.

You may apply to the B.A.L.S. program year-round and begin during the fall, winter, or spring term. The admission deadline for the fall term is August 1; for spring, December 1; and for summer, May 1. You must submit:

- The application form (This may be completed online or downloaded as a PDF for completion and mailed in. Either way, log on to http://scs.georgetown.edu/admissions/how-to-apply/bachelors-degrees#deadlines.)
- A $35 application fee
- A brief essay (about three pages, typewritten and double-spaced) describing what you have been doing since you were last a full-time student or explaining why you wish to enroll in the B.A.L.S. program
- Two letters of recommendation, from former professors and/or employers
- Official transcript(s), exams, and certifications
- TOEFL scores for those whose native language is not English

## TUITION AND HOUSING

Tuition for the summer and fall of 2012 was $905 per credit hour, or $2,715 per three-credit course and $3,620 per four-credit course. This amounts to a yearly tuition of about $25,000, assuming a full course load, which compares to $42,360 for undergraduates entering through the front gateway. On-campus housing for B.A.L.S. students is available on a limited basis. You should contact the school's Residential Life Office, which will either arrange on-campus housing for you or, more likely, direct you to off-campus housing opportunities.


For more information, contact:

Georgetown University
School of Continuing Studies
Office of Admissions
3307 M Street, NW, 2nd floor
Box 571006
Washington, DC 20057-1006
(202) 687-5942
Website: www.scs.georgetown.edu
Email: guadmiss@georgetown.edu

# 19

## Inland Flagship:
## University of Wisconsin-Madison

■ **KEYBOX**

**SCHOOL:** University of Wisconsin-Madison

**LOCATION:** Madison, Wisconsin

**COLLEGE RANKING:** 41

**GATE POSITION:** Wide open

**SAT REQUIRED:** Not always

**HOUSING:** Yes

**MINIMUM AGE:** <18

**APPLICATION CRITERIA:** Moderate

**MEDIAN STARTING SALARY:** $46,200

**COST COMPARED TO FRONT GATEWAY:** Varies

Flagship of the famously progressive Wisconsin university system, the Madison campus of the University of Wisconsin has long been a source of pride within the state and has also held a position of national renown for many years. The Carnegie Classification of Institutions of Higher Education categorizes Wisconsin-Madison as an RU/VH ("very high research activity") research university, with research expenditures topping a billion dollars for 2010. Only Johns Hopkins generates more research funds nationally, and no university's research is more diverse. Projects in some one hundred centers range from agriculture to the arts and from education to engineering. The university is a pioneer in embryonic stem cell research, a leader in research on internal combustion engines, and is one of only thirty U.S. sea grant colleges, with important programs in the conservation and productive use of American seacoasts and the Great Lakes.

Wisconsin-Madison is a big place, with twenty schools enrolling 30,367 undergraduates in 2012–2013. Full-time faculty tops two thousand; the institution offers 135 undergraduate majors as well as 151 master's and 107 doctoral programs. Although research and academics are in the forefront, Wisconsin Badger athletes compete in twenty-five intercollegiate sports within the Big 10. With all of this, UW-Madison occupies a solid position as one of the nation's so-called Public Ivies.

## THE WISCONSIN IDEA

Education has been a high priority in Wisconsin since it became a state in 1848, its leaders drawing up a constitution that explicitly called for "the establishment of a state university, at or near the seat of state government." The first class, seventeen students strong, convened in 1849 at the Madison Female Academy, and North Hall became the first building on the permanent campus in 1851.

In 1892, Charles R. Van Hise earned the first Ph.D. conferred by the university, and a dozen years later, in 1904, as the university's president, Dr. Hise presented what became known as the "Wisconsin Idea," declaring that he would "never be content until the beneficent influence of the University reaches every home in the state." His concept for the state's university was that its boundaries should not be defined by the limits of the campus, but by nothing less expansive than the boundaries of the state itself. This meant that the university should dedicate itself to research that would benefit all citizens. Not only did the Wisconsin Idea prove influential throughout the country, it formed the character of the Madison-based institution that continues to define it today: the notion that the university is no ivory tower, but, rather, an integral part of the community dedicated to its advancement and well-being.

## WISCONSIN CAMPUS LIFE TODAY

If you don't like frigid winters, UW-Madison may not be for you. January lows average in the single digits, and highs rarely rise above freezing during much of the winter. Record lows? Thirty-eight below zero one February day. Madison is by no means Siberia, however. The town is an architectural gem, and the hilly 933-acre campus, situated along the southern shore of Lake Mendota, near the state capitol, provides access to Madison's sophisticated small-town atmosphere while promoting a Big 10–campus lifestyle. As the *Princeton Review* points out, students enjoy opportunities to choose from among "every major under the sun, every kind of club, every kind of activity you can imagine."

With 135 undergraduate majors on offer, the sheer volume of choices can be daunting, but the university paves the way with counseling, guidance, and other programs aimed at facilitating the newcomer's transition to life at a major university. In fact, academic support services abound on the Madison campus, including, among other things, a writing center, a math tutorial program, a disability resource center, and programs designed especially for low-income and first-generation college students. The Exploration Center for Majors and Careers helps students who are just beginning to consider their specialty or are rethinking their choice of a major; career guidance of all sorts is available (and highly recommended) from the very moment a student first sets foot on campus. If you are a sports enthusiast, you will feel very much at home at UW-Madison, where students tend to be rabid Badger fans, who show special loyalty to the university's standout teams in football, hockey, and track.

## THE BACK GATEWAY TO UW-MADISON

As a "Public Ivy," UW-Madison makes for a formidably attractive bargain. In-state tuition and fees were $10,384 for 2012–2013, and out-of-state tuition, $26,634. Compare this to the $40,000-plus per-year price tag of most private elite universities. (Whether in-state or out-of-state, you will need to add $8,080 for room and board.)

Little wonder that some twenty-five thousand students applied for admission during 2012—more than 90 percent of them in the top quarter of their high school class. Madison officials accepted 50.5 percent. This makes the odds of getting through the front gateway a sliver better than fifty-fifty, but it also means that almost half those who apply are turned away. If you are in that latter half, why not try the back gateway?

It is accessed through the university's Guaranteed Transfer Program, which allows direct transfers from any of the thirteen University of Wisconsin colleges located throughout the state, in Baraboo/Sauk County, Barron County, Fond du Lac, Fox Valley, Manitowoc, Marathon County, Marinette, Marshfield/Wood County, Richland, Rock County, Sheboygan, Washington County, and Waukesha. The Guaranteed Transfer Program is open to Wisconsin residents and nonresidents alike. To qualify, you must:

1. Begin your education as a freshman at one of the UW Colleges.
2. Prior to your sophomore year, submit to UW–Madison's Office of Admissions a Declaration of Intent to Participate (go to www .admissions.wisc.edu/transfer/agrmnt_uwColleges.php), before completing thirty credits at your UW Colleges campus.
3. Complete 54 *transferable* (that is, non-remedial) credits at a UW Colleges campus within three years of your initial enrollment. (You must maintain enrollment at the UW Colleges during this period.)

4. Earn at least a 2.8 cumulative GPA and a 2.0 GPA for the term immediately prior to transfer.
5. Meet the minimum requirements for admission to UW–Madison, which include one year of high school algebra; one year of high school, college-track plane geometry; one year of college preparatory math (high school or equivalent); and two high school years or two college semesters of a single foreign language.

## How to Apply

You may apply online for transfer admission to UW-Madison at https://apply.wisconsin.edu. Be aware that February 1 is the application deadline for fall/summer terms, and October 1 for spring term. Depending on the major you intend to pursue, you may have to satisfy additional academic requirements or apply directly to an academic program. Note that certain majors, including teacher education, nursing, engineering, and business, require specific prerequisite courses, a higher grade point average (nursing, for instance, requires a 2.75 GPA, while some other programs call for a 3.0), and a separate application process. Log on to the UW-Madison Entrance Requirements for Majors web page, at www.wisc.edu/pubs/ug/entrance, for detailed information.

Whatever program you choose, once you have fulfilled specified "credit and Grade Point Average requirements," you will "transfer with the same rights and privileges as those who begin their education at" UW-Madison. The great thing about the program is that it offers a fully legitimate degree path for students who otherwise would not qualify for freshman admission to Madison. There are no age limits for prospective students, and whereas, in 2009–2010, 57 percent of incoming freshmen were in the top tenth of their high school class and 91 percent in the top 25 percent, most of the other colleges in the Wisconsin system will admit students in the top 75 percent of their class. Although you will not need SAT scores to transfer into UW-Madison, most of the UW Colleges themselves do require submission of standardized test scores prior to registration for classes.

## UW-MADISON CONNECTIONS PROGRAM

Most students who apply through the Guaranteed Admission Program will complete their application during their sophomore year at one of the UW Colleges; however, for in-state residents only, the university also offers the streamlined UW-Madison Connections Program. Admission into the program is limited to select college *freshmen* who agree to attend a partner college or university for their first two years, then finish their last two years at Madison. As the Connections Program website explains, this provides the opportunity to "hold the distinctive UW-Madison student status from the beginning," even though you attend another campus. Being a Connections student entitles you to receive, at the time of enrollment in the program in your freshman year, a Wiscard, the university's official student identification card. This gives you full access to the Madison campus libraries, health services, recreational facilities, and other campus services, including academic advising, student organizations, an array of technology tools, as well as access to Badger athletic events at a discount and other student ticket-package opportunities. Partner campuses include the following two-year colleges:

UW–Baraboo/Sauk County
UW–Barron County
UW–Fond du Lac
UW–Fox Valley
UW–Manitowoc
UW–Marathon County
UW–Marinette

UW–Marshfield/Wood County
UW–Richland
UW–Rock County
UW–Sheboygan
UW–Washington County
UW–Waukesha
Madison Area Technical College
Milwaukee Area Technical College
Nicolet Area Technical College
College of Menominee Nation

Also participating are five four-year campuses:

UW–Green Bay
UW–Parkside
UW–River Falls
UW–Stevens Point
UW–Stout

There are three ways to enter the Connections program:

1. **Connections Apply Direct:** If you are a Wisconsin resident and know you would like to begin at a partner campus and then transfer to UW-Madison, you may apply directly to the program. Complete the online Connections Intent to Apply Direct form at www.admissions.wisc.edu/connections/form.php. Next, apply simultaneously to UW–Madison and to the partner campus of your choice. Note that you must have completed all required high school coursework for UW-Madison freshman admission (four years of English; three years each of math, social studies, and science; and two years of a single foreign language), and you must have official results from the SAT or ACT (including the standardized writing test).

2. **Connections Opt-In:** If you applied as a freshman to UW-Madison and were accepted, you may still opt into Connections by choosing to complete your first two years of course work at a partner campus before transferring to the UW-Madison campus as a junior.

3. **Connections Invitation:** Because UW-Madison cannot accommodate all qualified students who apply, the Admissions Committee invites select applicants to participate in the Connections Program in lieu of direct freshman admission. These invitations are sent to applicants in mid-March, after all freshman applications have been reviewed.

## YET MORE FLEXIBILITY

Many of the two-year and four-year colleges in the Wisconsin system offer distance learning programs that allow students to take courses online and through video conferencing. Admission requirements vary widely by school and by program, but it is entirely possible to earn transferrable credits entirely online and thereby complete the requirements for a Guaranteed Transfer exclusively through online courses.

## TUITION AND HOUSING

Junior and senior years at UW-Madison carry tuition charges identical to those conventional front gateway students pay. The cost of your freshman and sophomore years, however, depends on your choice of UW College or partner institution. Check out the website for each institution you are considering, or contact an admissions counselor directly to determine the tuition rates for each particular gateway. Over the entire two-plus-two years of your education, it is likely that you will save some tuition costs compared to a full four years at Madison.

As for housing, most transfer students choose to live in non-university housing on the outskirts of campus; nevertheless, the university has designated one on-campus residence, Tripp Hall, for incoming transfer students. If you are interested, apply for space early. Check out the Division of University Housing website at www.housing.wisc.edu.

For more information, contact:

University of Wisconsin-Madison
500 Lincoln Drive
Madison, WI 53706
(608) 262-3961
Website: www.wisc.edu
Email: onwisconsin@admissions.wisc.edu

For the Guaranteed Transfer program, log on to www.admissions.wisc
.edu/transfer/agreements.php.

For the University of Wisconsin-Madison Connections Program, log on to www.admissions.wisc.edu/connections/index.php.

For more information on online learning throughout the Wisconsin system, log on to http://distancelearning.wisconsin.edu/index.cfm.

# 20

# A Metropolitan Education:
# New York University

> ■ **KEYBOX**
>
> **SCHOOL:** New York University
>
> **LOCATION:** New York, New York
>
> **COLLEGE RANKING:** 32
>
> **GATE POSITION:** Wide open
>
> **SAT REQUIRED:** No
>
> **HOUSING:** Yes
>
> **MINIMUM AGE:** 19
>
> **APPLICATION CRITERIA:** Moderate
>
> **MEDIAN STARTING SALARY:** $49,600
>
> **COST COMPARED TO FRONT GATEWAY:** Same

The 2013 edition of *U.S. News & World Report*'s *Best Colleges* ranks NYU number thirty-two nationwide, but Global Universities Ranking (www.globaluniversitiesranking.org) put it at a lofty number twenty-two internationally in 2009, and Academic Ranking of World Universities (www.arwu.org) ranked it thirty-third worldwide in 2010. Even more tellingly, NYU counts among its alumni and present and past faculty thirty-three Nobel laureates, sixteen Pulitzer Prize winners, and nineteen Oscar, Emmy, Grammy, and Tony winners. Notable graduates include senator, secretary of war, secretary of state, and 1912 Nobel

Peace Prize winner Elihu Root; former New York mayor and presidential candidate Rudy Giuliani; former Fed chairman Alan Greenspan; former FBI Director Louis Freeh; Congressmen Charles Rangel of New York and Christopher Shays of Connecticut; Southern gothic writer Carson McCullers; *Angela's Ashes* novelist Frank McCourt; comic Broadway playwright Neil Simon; and such business leaders as Richard Fuld, Leonard Stern, Laurence Tisch, and Barnes & Noble chairman Leonard Riggio.

Recently, the *Fiske Guide to Colleges* called the school "the hottest place in higher education," and for three years in a row, from 2004 to 2007, *Princeton Review* designated NYU as "America's #1 dream school" among high school seniors. Although in 2008 it slipped to fourth place in the "dream" ranking, behind Harvard, Yale, and Stanford (all of which offered better financial aid packages), *Newsweek* in 2006 placed NYU among twenty-five of what it called the "New Ivies." Few would begrudge it this distinction today.

## BIG SCHOOL IN THE VILLAGE

Manhattan's Greenwich Village has a history of bohemian artists and freethinkers occupying walk-ups and studio apartments, and today offers an array of tiny one-of-a-kind boutiques and pricey hole-in-the-wall restaurants. It is not a place you'd expect to be home to one of the largest private universities in the country, and yet NYU sprawls across 229 acres, from the southern border of the Village, at Houston Street, to its northern limit at Fourteenth Street, enfolding stately Washington Square Park at its center. For that matter, the university of today extends far beyond Greenwich Village, its eighteen schools, colleges, and institutes distributed in six locations throughout Manhattan and Brooklyn, with more units located as far away as London, Paris, Florence, Prague, Madrid, Berlin, Accra, Shanghai, Buenos Aires, Tel

Aviv, Singapore, Abu Dhabi, and—as of 2012—Washington, DC. More than nineteen thousand undergraduates are enrolled at the Greenwich Village campus, along with a like number of graduate students. Faculty numbers approach seven thousand, with administrative staff adding some fifteen thousand more. While many students live off campus, approximately 12,500 rely on university housing, making the NYU housing system the largest among U.S. private universities and the seventh-largest overall.

Of NYU's eighteen colleges, schools, and institutes, the College of Arts and Science is by far the largest academic division and consists of the College of Arts and Science, the Graduate School of Arts and Science, and a unit called Liberal Studies. Also open to undergraduates are the Gallatin School of Individualized Study; School of Social Work; Steinhardt School of Culture, Education and Human Development; Stern School of Business; and Tisch School of the Arts. In 1973, NYU merged its School of Engineering with Polytechnic University of New York, which in turn merged in 2008 with NYU and is now its Polytechnic Institute, the NYU engineering school. Graduate and professional programs also abound: at the College of Dentistry, College of Nursing, Courant Institute of Mathematical Sciences, Institute of Fine Arts, Institute for the Study of the Ancient World, Polytechnic Institute, School of Continuing and Professional Studies, School of Law, School of Medicine, Graduate School of Arts and Science, and Wagner Graduate School of Public Service.

Many of NYU's academic programs and departments are considered among the very best in the nation, including philosophy, Italian, finance, mathematics, and theater. The Law School was recently ranked at number six nationwide by *U.S. News & World Report*, and the Tisch School of the Arts has produced more Academy Award–winning alumni than any other film school in the United States. As for the heart of the institution, the Elmer Holmes Bobst Library is housed in a twelve-story Philip Johnson–Richard Foster building and boasts twenty-eight miles of open stacks, which contain most of the 4.5 million volumes in NYU's eight-library system—one of the largest academic libraries in the world.

New York University was the product of a literary and scientific conference convened in 1830 at City Hall. Here, more than a hundred delegates hammered out a plan to create in Manhattan a university modeled on what was then the radical new University of London, which had opened just four years earlier with the purpose of giving young men of academic promise a place to study regardless of their social status. The founders wanted to create for America a democratic institution of higher learning. With this in mind, they solicited public funding from the city and state, only to be turned down flat. Undaunted, the leaders of the movement to found the university—all prominent New Yorkers—raised $100,000 on their own and enticed former treasury secretary Albert Gallatin to serve as president.

The University of the City of New York was chartered by the state legislature on April 21, 1831, and was not officially renamed New York University until 1896. The first class was called into session in 1832, the students gathering in some rented rooms near City Hall. The university's School of Law opened three years later.

Difficult as it may be to imagine today, when NYU is a "dream school" whose students (or their parents) pay $40,878 a year in tuition, the university, along with much of New York City, fell on hard times during the late 1960s and early 1970s. Seeking to ward off imminent financial collapse, President James McNaughton Hester sold the University Heights campus to the City University of New York (CUNY) in 1973 and once again consolidated undergraduate operations in Greenwich Village. A massive and successful fund-raising campaign was launched in the 1980s to modernize and expand the university's physical plant, and in 2003 a new campaign raised some $2.5 billion to provide resources for faculty and to provide more financial aid to students.

## A MAGNET THAT JUST MAY RESIST YOU

"Don't count on getting into NYU just because Big Sis did," warns the *Fiske Guide to Colleges*. "The siren song of Greenwich Village has lured applications by the thousands." But it's not just the glamour of the Big Apple and the charm of the Village. The meteoric rise of many NYU departments and programs to national and international prominence and prestige has also been a very powerful draw.

In 2011–2012, 41,243 students—more than 60 percent in the top tenth of their high school class, more than 90 percent in the top quarter—applied, and 13,487 were accepted. With front gates open to some 32.7 percent, NYU is ranked among the "most selective" universities by *U.S. News*.

If you are among the seven out of ten students turned away from NYU, keep on turning—until you get to the university's back gateway.

## NYU'S BACK GATEWAY

Many who have endured the sting of exclusion from NYU must feel they have just cause to lament the apparent passing of the founders' promise of an open, democratic university. The truth is, however, that the Paul McGhee Division of NYU's School of Continuing and Professional Studies partakes even today of the progressive egalitarian spirit of 1830.

One of eight units of the School of Continuing and Professional Studies, the Paul McGhee Division offers courses designed to accommodate the schedules of working adults. While most classes are held in the evening, students do have the option of attending full- or part-time. You must be at least nineteen years old to apply, and be at least one year out of high school.

McGhee offers bachelor's and associate's degrees:

Bachelor of arts in humanities
- Concentration in art history
- Concentration in creative writing
- Concentration in literature

Bachelor of arts in social sciences
- Concentration in anthropology
- Concentration in economics
- Concentration in history
- Concentration in international studies
- Concentration in media studies
- Concentration in organizational behavior and communication
- Concentration in politics
- Concentration in psychology
- Concentration in sociology

Bachelor of science in digital communications and media

Bachelor of science in healthcare management

Bachelor of science in information systems management

Bachelor of science in leadership and management studies

Bachelor of science in real estate

Associate in arts in liberal arts

Associate in applied science in business

Associate in applied science in health administration

Associate in applied science in information systems management

Each degree carries its own requirements, but all students, once they are admitted, take a common core curriculum that includes:

- Writing (8–10 credits)
- Critical thinking (4 credits)
- Quantitative reasoning (4 credits)
- Scientific issues (4 credits)
- History, culture, and art (12 credits)

All students enrolled at McGhee are entitled to academic support at the writing center that serves all NYU undergraduates. They may also attend ongoing workshops devoted to such topics as research, presentation skills, and computer competence. Faculty advisors provide one-on-one assistance, and a dedicated academic advising program at the McGhee Division is especially designed to support new students without previous college experience or who enter the school with fewer than fifteen transferable credits. Moreover, if you find yourself undecided about what to major in, you can enroll as an "undeclared student"—a student who has yet to declare a major. You will work with an advisor to choose courses from the Core Curriculum and from the required courses of degree programs that interest you. After earning twenty to thirty credits, you must declare a major, and all of your credits will be transferred to the program you finally select.

In addition to academic counseling, McGhee provides support for career development through its Office of Career Management. Here, you will find individual career counseling as well as workshops to help you formulate a job search plan, develop an effective résumé, and sharpen your interviewing skills.

Bachelor's degrees through McGhee require 128 to 130 credits and associate's degrees 60 to 62 credits. Credits earned at another accredited college or university may be transferable up to 64 credits toward a bachelor's degree and 32 credits for an associate's. Subject to discussion with your academic advisor after you are accepted, you may also be given academic credit for your relevant "life experience."

While most classes are held in the evening at NYU's Washington Square campus (and are generally small, numbering twenty-five students or fewer), McGhee also offers an array of online learning programs. If you complete between forty and sixty-four credits at McGhee or at another regionally accredited university or college, you may be able to complete online a B.A. in social sciences with a concentration in organizational behavior and communication or a B.S. in leadership and management studies with a concentration in international business, human resource management, or organizational management and development. In consultation with your academic advisor, you may also be able to integrate online coursework into many other programs of study, including those for the B.A. in social sciences, B.S. in healthcare management, B.S. in real estate, B.S. in leadership and management studies, and A.A.S. in business.

## How to Apply

Everything you need to apply to NYU's Paul McGhee Division is available online at www.scps.nyu.edu/admissions/mcghee/apply. The Admissions Committee understands that applicants to the division come from a wide variety of backgrounds "and have unique interests and goals." For this reason, they use a "holistic approach" to evaluate each applicant's "ability to benefit from, and contribute to, the robust learning environment that McGhee offers." The committee's "admission decision is based on a collective review of all . . . application materials." These materials include:

- **Application form:** You may submit it online or download, print, and complete it on paper.
- **Résumé:** You should carefully detail your work and/or volunteer experience and your creative accomplishments.
- **Personal statement:** You are asked to write an essay of at least 350 typed words "that describes anything about you that you think we should know."
- **Letters of recommendation:** You'll need to send two from people who know you through academic, professional, or volunteer experience.
- **Official transcripts:** You must send an official transcript from each college or university you have attended. (After you are ad-

mitted, you *may* also be required to submit an official high school transcript.)

The Admissions Committee looks in particular for students who "are proactive individuals who take meaningful roles in charting their educational and career plans and who demonstrate the characteristics and evidence of abilities that are likely to contribute to their success as undergraduate students at McGhee."

- Committee members review your résumé to assess how your "professional, personal, and/or volunteer experiences . . . may shape your educational and career goals and enrich the educational process." The accomplishments and responsibilities you choose to highlight "may also serve as useful demonstration of your motivation, maturity, and focus."
- Your personal statement serves to create "a better understanding of your background as well as your interests." The committee also uses it to "evaluate your writing ability and potential."
- Your letters of recommendation "provide . . . a view of your skills and qualifications for college-level study through the perspective of individuals who know you through either professional or academic connections." You are encouraged to share with recommenders "some information about the McGhee Division . . . so they can tailor their recommendations appropriately."
- Any college transcripts you submit will be "reviewed for insight into past academic experiences." You are invited also to bring to the attention of the Admission Committee any information "that may be relevant to your academic history, including prior performance or a postponement of your education."

Applications are accepted and reviewed throughout the year on a rolling basis, subject to the following deadlines:

- For admission to the fall term, the recommended deadline for submission of all application materials is July 1 and the final date is August 15.
- For spring term, November 1 is recommended, December 15 is final.
- For summer term, April 1 is recommended, May 1 is final.

## TUITION AND HOUSING

For 2012, tuition at McGhee for full-time students was $9,627 per term. You will be required to purchase health insurance if you don't already have appropriate coverage; for 2012–2013, the annual basic-plan premium was $2,150. Financial aid is available for undergraduate students in the McGhee Program, who may apply for scholarships and loans based on financial need and academic merit.

It is important to know that university housing is "very limited" and available only to full-time students who are enrolled for at least twelve credits each semester. If you plan to attend full-time and want to live on campus, you must submit a housing application to the Office of Admissions by the priority deadline for the fall term.

Part-time students cannot live on campus and must instead secure off-campus housing. But even for full-time students, the demand for on-campus housing always exceeds the supply, so that the Office of Admissions "strongly suggests" that even full-time McGhee students seek non-university housing and visit the NYU Office of Off-Campus Housing to secure assistance in finding a place to live. (Such assistance is available only after you have been admitted to NYU.)

For more information, contact:

New York University
School of Continuing and Professional Studies

Office of Admissions
Paul McGhee Division
145 Fourth Avenue, Room 219
New York, NY 10003
General information: (212) 998-7200 or (888) 998-7204
Degree admissions: (212) 998-7100
Website: www.scps.nyu.edu/admissions/mcghee.html
Email: scps.info@nyu.edu

# 21

## Engineering Your Entrance into the University of Southern California

---

■ **KEYBOX**

**SCHOOL:** University of Southern California

**LOCATION:** Los Angeles, California

**COLLEGE RANKING:** 24

**GATE POSITION:** Half-open

**SAT REQUIRED:** No

**HOUSING:** Yes

**MINIMUM AGE:** 18

**APPLICATION CRITERIA:** Moderate

**MEDIAN STARTING SALARY:** $54,600

**COST COMPARED TO FRONT GATEWAY:** Varies

---

L ike many other things in Los Angeles, a USC education is a pricey proposition—$44,463 in tuition and fees for 2012–2013, plus $12,440 for room and board—but, also like much that Southern California has to offer, a USC education is in high demand. The raw numbers say as much: In 2012, 23 percent of those who applied were accepted. Dig a little deeper into the numbers, and you will discover the remarkable fact that, despite the high cost, USC is the nation's third most economically diverse top-ranked school. The conclusion is obvious. Students *really* want to study here.

The campus is beautiful. The central L.A. location is exciting. The pre-professional programs are very strong, and USC's identity as a research powerhouse is both well established and growing. School spirit among alumni is legendary. Alums not only call themselves "Trojans"—after the university's highly ranked sports teams—they proclaim themselves "Trojans for life." If you think this implies that alumni networks are helpful in getting new graduates great jobs, you're right. But the same networks that promote careers also influence who gets through the front gate and who does not. Fully 22 percent of admissions are influenced by "legacy preferences." This means that unless you have a family connection to USC, your chances of getting in, slim enough at one in four, may be even slimmer.

Good thing there's a back gateway.

## ACADEMIC DISTINCTION

The University of Southern California was founded through the tireless efforts of a visionary jurist, Robert M. Widney, judge of the Court of California for Los Angeles and San Bernardino Counties, who solicited funds from a diverse group of donors united mainly by their shared prominence in the civic life of late-nineteenth-century Los Angeles. Horticulturalist Ozro Childs was active in the Methodist Church; John Gately Downey, a former governor, was equally active in the Roman Catholic faith; and Isaiah Hellman, a successful local banker, was well known as a leader of Southern California's small Jewish community. Together, the three donated 308 land lots for the campus and ponied up funding for construction of the first university buildings. Childs then secured the sponsorship of the Methodist Church (the affiliation did not officially end until 1952), but neither religion, race, nor gender would ever serve as cause to deny admission.

When USC opened its doors in 1880, Los Angeles was a dusty, unpaved town with neither electricity nor telephones. Today, the campus is in the heart of a great city, adjacent to the downtown business district, and is the single largest private employer in Los Angeles. At 235 acres, University Park has been described as an urban oasis. The older buildings that rise from the cobbled lanes and manicured campus lawns are Romanesque in style, whereas the new buildings represent a variety of the best in Modernist design. And while students doubtless enjoy their oasis, more than half of them regularly volunteer to do public work in the surrounding neighborhood, much of which is both underprivileged and underserved.

USC is and always was good for L.A. and for Southern California, annually contributing some $4 billion to the local economy, but by the 1960s, it had clearly fallen out of step with the generally liberal tenor of California politics and soon developed a reputation as a bastion of political conservatism. Today, however, the campus is once again known for its diverse liberalism of social, cultural, and political thought.

Notable alumni include postmodern architect Frank Gehry; former Citigroup chairman Charles Prince; astronauts Neil Armstrong and Walter Schirra; former secretary of state Warren Christopher; NASA administrator Michael Griffin; Securities and Exchange Commission chairman Christopher Cox; the late humorist Art Buchwald; Tijuana Brass trumpeter Herb Alpert; actors John Wayne, Forrest Whitaker, Tom Selleck, and Will Ferrell; Hollywood studio moguls Jack Warner and Darryl Zanuck; and filmmaker George Lucas.

Academic distinction and a well-connected alumni network have given USC an amply merited reputation as an on-ramp for fast-track entry into the elite Southern California business and professional communities. Long known as a great place for pre-med and pre-law undergrads, USC has received a recent influx of nine-figure gifts, which it used to create and expand the Annenberg Center for Communication, build the Alfred E. Mann Institute for Biomedical Engineering, and expand the School of Medicine. A $175 million gift from *Star Wars* creator George Lucas substantially expanded the existing USC School of Cinema-Television into what is now called the USC School of Cinematic Arts. In addition, recent years have seen the Viterbi School of Engineering consistently ranked among the top ten graduate engineering schools in the country. With 1,800 undergraduates—7 percent of USC's total undergraduate enrollment—in addition to 3,800 graduate students, Viterbi is known as the "Cradle of the Digital Age" for its role in developing the digital technology that has revolutionized the way the world communicates.

## THE VITERBI ALTERNATIVE

If enrolling in USC is usually a one-in-four proposition—and, thanks to the role of legacy admissions, probably an even longer shot for most—transferring into USC is even more highly competitive and selective. Not only do you need a 3.7 GPA, but only about one in eight students applying for transfer are admitted.

If it looks to you as if USC actively discourages transfers, maybe you're right. But there is one school that aggressively seeks them, and it is a great school. "Transfer students are an important element in the creative and diverse mix of students at the Viterbi School of Engineering," school officials proclaim. They point out that "more than 20 percent of our undergraduate community transferred to USC from two- or four-year schools."

## THE TWO-YEAR TRANSFER

Viterbi offers streamlined transfer to students of the more than one hundred California two-year community colleges. The Viterbi faculty has clearly thought long and hard about such transfers and offers transfer planning guides (TPGs) that are specifically tailored to the prospective transferee's major and institution. If you are interested, log on to http://viterbi.usc.edu/admission/transfer/guides.htm for links to the

TPG that's appropriate for you. Even if you cannot find your institution listed on the TPG website, you can still apply for a transfer. To prepare, you will be asked to check the "USC Articulation Histories" (at https://camel2.usc.edu/articagrmt/artic_hist_range.aspx) and contact an admission advisor at Viterbi (http://viterbi.usc.edu/admission/contact.htm).

Although each TPG lists individual requirements for transferring from a particular institution, you should know that, generally speaking, you will be expected to have earned a minimum of thirty transferable credits, compiled a GPA of 3.0 or higher in doing so, and completed as many core engineering courses as possible before you apply for transfer. As a transfer applicant, you will also have to satisfy the USC writing requirement by successfully completing a course equivalent to USC's second-semester composition course and (in most cases) also taking two English composition courses before transferring. Although USC also has general education requirements for graduation, Viterbi does not require transfer students to complete these prior to admission. Once admitted, however, you will be required to take one course in each of six areas: Western cultures and traditions, global cultures and traditions, scientific inquiry, science and its significance, arts and letters, and social issues.

## THE 3/2 PROGRAM

The Viterbi School of Engineering has established 3/2 programs with some forty four-year liberal arts colleges, not just in California but across the country. If you enroll in a Viterbi 3/2 program, you will earn two bachelor's degrees in five years, one in a liberal arts field and one in engineering. Most 3/2 students study during their first three years at a partner liberal arts institution and then transfer to USC, where they spend two years completing their engineering program.

To obtain a list of the current 3/2 partner institutions and secure a

"3/2 Agreement Guide," visit http://viterbi.usc.edu/admission/transfer/ threetwo.htm and click on the email link to a "Viterbi transfer admission counselor." The "3/2 Agreement Guide" specifies the courses you will need to take at your partner institution before you transfer to USC. It also lays out the engineering course work you will undertake after the transfer. While specific course work requirements vary by major and partner institution, you should know that most 3/2 program students take the following before they transfer:

- **General education courses:** Requirements vary by school.
- **Mathematics courses:** Requirements vary by school and engineering major, but most students complete calculus I, II, III, linear algebra, and/or differential equations.
- **Physics courses:** Requirements vary by major; however, the sequence should address thermodynamics, mechanics, electricity, magnetism, optics, and modern physics.
- **Chemistry courses:** Requirements vary by major, but most students take general chemistry I and II, and chemical and biomedical engineers must also take organic chemistry before transferring.
- **Computer programming courses:** Computer engineering and industrial and systems majors should take C++, and all other majors need MATLAB.
- **Writing courses:** At least one semester of lower-division writing is required prior to transfer.
- If your partner institution offers additional engineering course work, you should take as much as possible before transferring.

As with transfers from two-year institutions, you will be expected to complete your course work at the partner institution with a 3.0 cumulative GPA.

It is critically important that you contact a Viterbi admissions counselor to obtain the latest information on 3/2 partnerships, since USC admissions officials note that participating schools do change. Recent partner institutions have included the likes of Pepperdine University, University of Puget Sound, Willamette University, Colorado College, Lewis & Clark College, and Whittier College.

## How to Apply

Whether you are transferring from a two-year California college or from a 3/2 partner institution, you will need to submit the Part II Application for Admission by the application deadline, which is February 1. You may complete Part II online at www.usc.edu/admission/undergraduate /apply/transfer.html. This same website also contains links to a downloadable version of the application, which you may (if you prefer) fill out in hard copy and submit by mail. As part of your Part II application, you must also submit official transcripts from all colleges attended after high school graduation along with official high school transcripts.

In addition to the Part II Application for Admission, which is required of all transfer applicants, 3/2 students must also submit the Viterbi Supplemental Application, which is available at http://viterbi.usc.edu/ admission/transfer/application. Transferees from two-year institutions are not *required* to complete the Viterbi Supplemental Application, but it is strongly recommended that they do so as well. Transferees participating in the 3/2 program must also submit a letter of support from their institution's 3/2 advisor.

The Viterbi School Admissions Committee explains that transfer decisions are made "through a comprehensive review of the entire admission application," but the "most influential factors are previous academic performance in challenging classes and demonstrated success in engineering and engineering related classes such as advanced math and science." For this reason, as you prepare for transfer, be sure to take advantage of the tutoring and study skills assistance that are available through Viterbi's Academic Resource Center. You must also meet with your designated academic advisor at least once each semester.

## TUITION AND HOUSING

Tuition rates vary, depending on what program you choose, but once you are actually enrolled at USC you can count on having to pay tuition costs that are at least roughly equivalent to what nontransfer students pay. If you transfer into USC from two-year California colleges or from participating 3/2 partners, you will pay the tuition charged by those institutions while you attend them. It is possible, therefore, that you will enjoy a substantial net savings over your entire college career.

Although USC tuition is formidable, the institution administers what it characterizes as a "robust financial aid program" that offers a range of financial aid, including need-based grants, merit scholarships, low-interest loans, and work-study programs. As the university website puts it, "USC has a long tradition of meeting 100 percent of the USC-determined financial need for those undergraduate students who satisfy all eligibility requirements and deadlines."

On-campus housing is not guaranteed to transfer students, who, if they want to live on campus, must submit a special application for what university housing "may be available." Admissions officials say that many transfer students choose to rent private housing instead of living on campus.

For more information, contact:

USC Viterbi School of Engineering
Office of Admission
Ronald Tutor Hall, Room 110
3710 South McClintock Avenue
Los Angeles, CA 90089-2900
(213) 740-4530 or (800) 526-3347
Email: viterbi.admission@usc.edu

# 22

# Campus on a Hill: Boston College

> ■ **KEYBOX**
>
> SCHOOL: Boston College
>
> LOCATION: Boston, Massachusetts
>
> COLLEGE RANKING: 31
>
> GATE POSITION: Wide open
>
> SAT REQUIRED: No
>
> HOUSING: Limited
>
> MINIMUM AGE: <18
>
> APPLICATION CRITERIA: Moderate
>
> MEDIAN STARTING SALARY: $51,500
>
> COST COMPARED TO FRONT GATEWAY: Half

It may call itself a *college*—that's what it was founded as back in 1863—but Boston College is actually a major research university with some 9,100 full-time undergraduates and nearly 5,000 graduate students, awarding bachelor's, master's, and doctoral degrees in nine schools and colleges. Like Georgetown University in Washington, DC, Boston College is a private Roman Catholic Jesuit institution, with an educational program that reflects what college officials call a four-hundred-year Jesuit "tradition of concern for the integration of the intellectual, moral, and religious development of its students." Thus, undergraduate education at Boston College is organized around a common core curriculum "that emphasizes the study of the defining works of the humanities, natural sciences, and social sciences."

If the curriculum honors a traditional core, the campus itself is an architectural icon of collegiate traditionalism. Located in the village of Chestnut Hill, six miles west of downtown Boston, the 175-acre central campus includes more than 120 buildings, most of them designed and built early in the twentieth century in the Collegiate Gothic style by architect Charles Donagh Maginnis. He envisioned the school's hilltop location as an opportunity to build in modern America the "city upon a hill" Jesus spoke of in his Sermon on the Mount: "You are the light of the world. A city that is set on a hill cannot be hidden." The magnificent campus is listed on the National Register of Historic Places.

## OPEN-MINDED STUDENTS WITH
## A PHILOSOPHICAL INFLUENCE

If you are thinking of applying, you're not alone. Rated "most selective" by *U.S. News & World Report* in *Best Colleges 2013*, the institution accepted 28 percent of applicants in 2012. This means, of course, that nearly three-fourths of those who came knocking at the front gateway were turned back. As you will see, however, there *is* a back gateway, and it is substantially wider than the front one.

But first, a little history.

Boston College was founded by the Society of Jesus in 1863 primarily to provide an excellent education to the sons of the many Irish immigrants living in and around Boston. When it opened its doors on September 5, 1864, there were twenty-two students and three teachers. For the next seventy years, the school remained a small undergraduate institution devoted to teaching theology, philosophy, the Greek and Latin classics, and English and modern languages to a predominantly working-class Irish Roman Catholic student body. Back then, the college was located not on Chestnut Hill, but in the densely populated, heavily Irish South End of Boston. Early in the twentieth century, as the school's reputation for excellence spread, it outgrew its urban campus and moved to what had been the Lawrence family farm in bucolic Chestnut Hill. Ground was broken for the first building on June 19, 1909.

During the 1920s, Boston College developed into a genuine university, opening its Graduate School of Arts and Sciences, the Law School, and the Evening College—which is today the James A. Woods, S.J., College of Advancing Studies—before the end of the decade.

Boston College expanded further in 1974, acquiring a forty-acre site a mile and a half from the Chestnut Hill campus. Today, the Law School and freshman residence halls are located there. In 2004, land adjacent to the lower campus in Chestnut Hill was acquired to accommodate the School of Theology and Ministry, which was formed in 2008.

Noted alumni include Massachusetts senator and 2004 Democratic presidential candidate John Kerry, former Massachusetts governors Paul Celucci and Edward King, Boston mayors Kevin White and John F. "Honey Fitz" Fitzgerald—grandfather of President John F. Kennedy—legendary speaker of the House Thomas P. "Tip" O'Neill, and U.S. representatives Edward Boland, Ed Markey, Silvio Conte, and Robert Drinan.

Recent years have seen tremendous growth at Boston College, which in 2007 implemented a $1.6 billion plan to improve the campus and hire new faculty. This single comprehensive plan represents an investment nearly equal to the university's impressive endowment of $1.726 billion. The expansion has been in response to increased undergraduate applications, which have grown by more than 40 percent during the past decade, and while Boston College denies adhering to any set admissions formula, its Admission Committee does look for applicants who are "passionate and make connections between academic pursuits and extracurricular activities." A lofty GPA is not enough to get you in. As the *Princeton Review* observes, "The application process should reveal a distinct, mature voice and a student whose interest in education goes beyond the simple desire to earn an 'A.'" Nevertheless, the Boston College Admissions Office also stresses that "highly competitive SAT or ACT scores improved the chance of admission."

Although Boston College is one of the oldest Roman Catholic Jesuit universities in the United States, you certainly don't have to be Catholic to attend. One in three students is not, and only sixty of the institution's nine hundred faculty members are Jesuits. Admission is without regard to religion. All of this said, the *Fiske Guide to Colleges* observes that the Jesuit faculty minority exerts a philosophical influence "disproportionate" to its number. This means that Boston College resolutely aims to reflect the Jesuit ideals of "community, spirituality and social justice." In keeping with the Jesuit philosophy of educating the entire person, the university's required core curriculum includes:

One course in the arts
Two courses in history
One course in literature
One course in writing
One course in mathematics
Two courses in philosophy
Two courses in natural science
Two courses in social science
Two courses in theology
One course in cultural diversity

As one student puts it, the core curriculum forces you "to take classes you might not want to take, but end up enjoying," and another observes that "the philosophy, theology and ethics departments are the most important in setting the tone of the campus because they keep the students encouraged to be open-minded." The Boston College faculty presented a cogent and persuasive rationale for the core curriculum in a 1991 report, which is available at www.bc.edu/offices/avp/core

//structure.html#IV. If you're thinking about applying, you'll find the document eye-opening.

## THE BACK GATEWAY TO BOSTON COLLEGE

So what do you do if you want what Boston College has to offer but find yourself among the three out of four applicants who don't get invited in? Look to the James A. Woods, S.J., College of Advancing Studies, which offers a back gateway to bachelor's degrees in a wide range of fields.

"The admissions process is designed to respond to the strengths and needs of talented applicants from all walks of life," according to the Woods College website. As the Admissions Committee sees them, all Woods applicants "are unique, yet all share much in common, not the least of which is the desire to continue their education. Advancing Studies students are accepted, not for where they are, but where they want to go and what they might become." Although "secondary school graduation or an equivalency certificate is required" for admission, Woods College emphasizes that "entrance requirements are flexible." The Admissions Committee looks for evidence of "motivation, interest and present seriousness of purpose." There are no entrance examinations, not even a requirement for SAT or ACT scores. If you have completed some college work, you may even be granted advanced standing, provided that the courses you have taken are "equivalent in content and quality to those offered by Boston College" and you have achieved a grade of at least a C in them.

The bachelor of arts program offers "the atmosphere of a small college within the environment of a large university." You are promised personal attention as well as full access to the resources of a major research university. You may register for day or evening classes and may take a maximum of three courses per semester—although you can secure permission to take one additional course if you have completed your previous semester's work with a grade of B– or above in each course. If you are transferring from another institution, you must complete at least half of your course work at Woods College to receive a degree.

As is the case with front gateway students, regardless of your major, you will be required to complete a core curriculum, consisting of the courses in humanities, social sciences, mathematics, and sciences listed earlier in this chapter. Woods College students may choose from the following undergraduate majors:

- **American studies:** You will elect five courses in either American history or American literature, and select three courses from the other field.
- **Communication:** You will take survey of mass communication, public speaking, and a combination of eight additional communication courses.
- **Computer information technology:** In addition to statistics and a year of math, you will be required to complete six computer courses, including exploring the Internet, database management, and a second-level programming course.
- **Corporate systems:** This innovative major combines "theory, practice and an interest in management and social responsibility within the arts, business, criminal justice, information technology, education, health care, private, non-profit and public sectors." Degree requirements include two math courses and course work in a "professional studies area," such as accounting, communication, criminal and social justice, finance, information technology, management, or marketing.
- **Criminal and social justice:** This major is intended to help career personnel in law enforcement, juvenile service, social service, corrections, parole, and probation agencies to develop "greater analytical communication and leadership skill."

- **Economics:** In addition to core curriculum economics courses, you will take micro and macroeconomic theory, statistics, and six economic electives.
- **English:** This major is recommended for those interested in writing, whether commercial or creative; editorial work; public relations; corporate and academic teaching; advertising and business.
- **History:** In addition to core history requirements, the history major must complete eight history electives.
- **Political science:** Majors in this field typically prepare themselves for "political and administrative careers, foreign service, law, journalism and teaching in the social sciences."
- **Psychology:** You will be required to take introductory psychology, statistics and research methods, and six other psychology electives in addition to one year of mathematics, biology, or nutrition.
- **Social science:** Intended to develop "a general knowledge of contemporary society from a political, economic, historical and social perspective," this major offers students wide latitude in choosing courses from among economics, history, political science, psychology, and sociology.
- **Sociology:** This major is designed to prepare students for careers in sociology, social work, and related areas. In addition to introductory sociology, sociological theory, and statistics and methods of social research, you will take four additional sociology electives.

## How to Apply

Applicants to the Woods College of Advancing Studies are asked to complete an extraordinarily straightforward single-page application that you may download at www.bc.edu/content/bc/schools/advstudies/about/index.html. In addition, you must submit all of your high school and college transcripts. There is no age requirement or entrance exam, and neither the SAT nor the ACT is required. Remember: The Admissions Committee is most interested in your "motivation, interest and present seriousness of purpose" as "criteria for admission," so think carefully about how you write these two highly important portions of the application form:

Attach a brief paragraph commenting on your past academic record as an indication of your ability for advanced studies.

Briefly detail your present reasons for seeking further education and your planned career and life goals. Include any significant career, social, athletic or educational experiences.

Also be aware that you will be awarded credits for all equivalent college courses in which you have earned a grade of at least C. Additionally, the Woods College Admissions Committee evaluates "nontraditional learning" (including "life experience") for college credit on the basis of the College Level Examination Program (CLEP) test.

## TUITION AND HOUSING

Each one-semester undergraduate course at Woods College carries a tuition charge of $1,624 as of 2012–2013, and there is a registration fee of $20 per semester. In addition, mandatory Massachusetts medical insurance is required, at $2,290 annually, unless you already have equivalent or better coverage. A variety of financial aid packages, scholarships, and work-study opportunities are available.

On-campus housing is available only to those Woods College students who attend classes between June 29 and August 7. For the rest of the school year, you are on your own, except for whatever aid and guidance the Student Services Office may be able to provide in helping you to secure suitable off-campus housing.

For more information, contact:

James A. Woods College of Advancing Studies
Boston College
Chestnut Hill, MA 02467
Website: www.bc.edu/schools/advstudies

# 23

## Cutting-Edge Colonial:
## The College of William & Mary

■ **KEYBOX**

**SCHOOL:** The College of William & Mary

**LOCATION:** Williamsburg, Virginia

**COLLEGE RANKING:** 33

**GATE POSITION:** Wide open

**SAT REQUIRED:** Yes

**HOUSING:** Yes

**MINIMUM AGE:** 18

**APPLICATION CRITERIA:** Moderate

**MEDIAN STARTING SALARY:** $46,900

**COST COMPARED TO FRONT GATEWAY:** Less than half for the first two years

The faculty and students of the College of William & Mary proudly proclaim themselves "different." The school's name and eighteenth-century architecture suggest a small private college, but William & Mary is a *public* university with nearly six thousand undergraduates and more than two thousand graduate students, all served by some six hundred full-time faculty members. Founded in 1693 in Williamsburg, the capital of colonial Virginia, today much of its hometown is given over to a meticulous and very popular antique re-creation known as Colonial Williamsburg. Yet W&M is also a center of advanced research as well as the home of highly respected schools of law and medicine. The university takes pride in involving undergraduates in that research, and its overall twelve-to-one student-instructor ratio is the second lowest among U.S. public universities. Often called the "original Public Ivy," the College of William & Mary is an old school that has put itself on the cutting edge.

No wonder a lot of students want to be part of it. Ranked thirty-third overall nationally by *U.S. News & World Report* in *Best Colleges 2013*, W&M came in sixth among all *public* universities the year before, and *Times Higher Education* ranked it seventy-fifth worldwide in 2010. Of those who applied for admission by January 2012, 34.6 were accepted. When you consider that about 80 percent of all applicants were in the top tenth of their high school class and two-thirds of those accepted were Virginia residents, you can readily understand why W&M is classified as "most selective."

## DON'T KNOW YOUR MAJOR?
## DECIDE LATER OR DESIGN YOUR OWN

Chartered on February 8, 1693, by the monarchs of England's "Glorious Revolution," King William III and Queen Mary II, the school was the second institution of higher learning, after Harvard, founded in the American colonies. If Virginia is the "cradle of presidents," the College of William & Mary was often the hand that rocked that cradle. George Washington was not a student here, but he did receive his surveyor's certificate from the college at the tender age of seventeen. Thomas Jefferson was both a graduate and an instructor, and Presidents James Monroe and John Tyler were alumni, as was the fourth—and arguably most influential—chief justice of the U.S. Supreme Court, John Marshall. Congress's "Great Compromiser," Henry Clay; fourteenth U.S. vice president and fifth Confederate secretary of war

John C. Breckinridge; and General Winfield Scott, hero of the War of 1812, the U.S.-Mexican War, and general-in-chief of the Union Army at the outbreak of the Civil War, were students. More recent alumni include Pittsburgh Steelers head coach Mike Tomlin, actors Glenn Close and Scott Glenn, *The Daily Show* host Jon Stewart, fashion mogul Perry Ellis, U.S. secretary of defense Robert Gates, and NASA astronaut David M. Brown.

In 1928, the university gained national recognition when John D. Rockefeller Jr. chose the Wren Building—the oldest structure on the campus, named after the neoclassical British architect Sir Christopher Wren—as the first building to be restored in what would become Colonial Williamsburg. Throughout the 1930s, W&M expanded, and although graduate programs and research rose to prominence as university priorities, the focal point of the school remained, and has always remained, the undergraduate program with its high teacher-to-student ratio and "small college" feel. Since 1989, W&M has produced a half dozen Rhodes Scholars, and since 2000, sixty recipients of Fulbright Scholarships and Truman and Goldwater Fellowships. No major American research university has produced more Fulbright Scholars.

All W&M undergraduates take a general education core curriculum that is rooted in the College of Arts and Sciences and that is intended to provide an exploratory background in "the range of human knowledge across dozens of departments and programs." After completing this core and deciding on a major, students choose from programs in arts and sciences, the Mason School of Business, or the School of Education. In addition to traditional major fields, W&M offers an array of interdisciplinary majors, such as global studies, environmental studies, medieval and Renaissance studies, and black studies, and it is also possible to work with willing faculty members to design one's own major.

## THE BACK GATEWAY TO W&M

Two-thirds of those who apply to this extraordinary state school are turned away. Many of those who do not walk through the front gateway are residents of states other than Virginia—for the Admissions Committee does give some preference to residents. Fortunately, there is a back gateway, and it is wide open.

The Richard Bland College (RBC) of the College of William & Mary is a liberal arts junior college located fifty miles from Williamsburg, in the town of Petersburg. As the only public, two-year institution in Virginia that offers on-campus living facilities and as the only state-supported junior college, RBC bills itself as "the perfect choice for students looking for the full collegiate experience but at the significantly reduced cost of a junior college." The primary mission of RBC is to offer associate degree programs in liberal arts and sciences that are designed to be thoroughly transferable through guaranteed transfer agreements with fifteen four-year Virginia colleges, including William & Mary. In fact, RBC is a very well-used back gateway, as more than 90 percent of the school's associate degree graduates do transfer to four-year colleges to complete their bachelor's degrees.

Whereas W&M is "most selective," acceptance at RBC is "noncompetitive," and about 88 percent of applicants are admitted. That makes getting in a lot easier. And the tuition cost savings for the first two years of college makes paying for education easier, too. Two years' tuition at RBC costs less than half that of W&M.

RBC offers two associate degrees, one in arts (A.A.) and one in science (A.S.). The A.A. is designed primarily for students who plan to transfer and work toward a baccalaureate in a field of the arts, the humanities, or the social sciences. Typical areas of study that could be started under the RBC A.A. program and completed at W&M include:

| | |
|---|---|
| Art | Interior design |
| English and literature | Philosophy |
| Fine arts | Religion |
| Foreign languages | Theater and drama |
| History | Theology |

The A.S. is intended mainly for students who want to complete bachelor's degrees in education, business, health professions, social work, engineering, or one of the natural sciences. You might, for example, begin any of the following at RBC and complete a bachelor's degree at W&M:

| | |
|---|---|
| Accounting | Engineering |
| Anthropology | Finance |
| Astronomy | Government |
| Biological science | History |
| Business | International affairs |
| Chemistry | Journalism |
| Communication | Mathematics |
| Computer science | Physics |
| Criminal justice | Political science |
| Ecology | Psychology |
| Economics | Sociology |
| Education | |

Although most courses require regular class attendance, a limited number of RBC courses can be taken online.

## HOW TO APPLY TO RBC

To apply for admission to an RBC associate degree program, you must have graduated from an accredited high school or have earned an equivalency certificate based on GED tests. Although most applicants are admitted, all applications are individually evaluated on the basis of high school courses completed, the grades achieved in them, extracurricular activities, SAT scores, and, if you choose to include them in your application, personal recommendations.

As a rule, required high school course work includes four years of English, three of mathematics, two of history or government, two of science, and two of a foreign language. Your cumulative GPA should be a minimum of 2.00. If you are an international student, you must also have achieved a minimum score of 500 on the Test of English as a Foreign Language (TOEFL).

To apply to RBC, visit www.rbc.edu/admissions.php#applications to download the necessary application forms. These will also provide detailed application instructions. The main items required for application are:

- The completed application form
- A $25 application fee
- High school transcripts
- College transcripts (if any)
- SAT scores

The application form has space for two required essays, which "should be completed by the student without assistance." They may be typed or handwritten on the form or on separate paper. The first essay is to answer the question "Why would you like to attend Richard Bland College?" The second essay responds to "What other information should the Office of Admissions and Student Development know about you when considering your application?"

Letters of recommendation are not required, but the Admissions Committee will read and consider them if submitted.

The Admissions Committee encourages early application; however, applications are accepted throughout the year. Suggested deadlines are July 1 for the fall semester and November 1 for the spring semester.

## HOW TO APPLY FOR TRANSFER FROM RBC TO W&M

The formal transfer agreement in force between RBC and W&M guarantees your acceptance at W&M from RBC if you:

- Have completed the two-year associate degree with at least forty-five credits and a GPA of 3.0, excluding physical education ("It is best to have a 3.0 or better at the time of application," RBC officials advise.)
- Are a state resident (Nonresidents *may* be accepted for transfer, but are not *guaranteed* acceptance.)
- Have enrolled in courses that satisfy W&M's general education requirements (GER)

You should take RBC's History and Religion of Israel to satisfy W&M's history/culture outside the European tradition GER. An RBC course in art, theater, music, or speech will satisfy W&M's requirement in creative and performing arts. Either Introduction to Philosophy or Introduction to Ethics will satisfy W&M's philosophical, religious, and social thought GER. Although having completed these GER equivalents is not absolutely required for admission, doing so before you transfer means that you will not have to take the courses at W&M.

W&M officials also recommend that you complete your foreign language requirement before transferring, and you should take note of specific additional requirements if you intend to major in business administration; for these, see www.rbc.edu/williammary.php.

You may apply for the fall or the spring semester, and there are no age requirements.

## TUITION AND HOUSING

As of 2012–2013, a year of in-state tuition and fees at W&M ran $13,570, plus $9,318 for room and board, whereas a year at RBC carried a tuition bill of $3,658 for in-state commuter students and $4,384 tuition for in-state residential students, who must also pay $10,270 a year for room and board. Out-of-state tuition and fees at W&M were $36,752 (plus the same $9,318 for room and board) for 2012–2013. Out-of-state RBC commuter students paid $13,524 in tuition for 2012–2013. Residential out-of-state RBC students paid $14,250 for the year, in addition to the same room and board costs paid by in-state students.

Obviously, RBC students enjoy very significant costs savings over W&M students for the first two years of college, and, also obviously, in-state students pay much less than out-of-state students. At the time of your application to RBC, you will be asked to fill out an in-state residency form, which determines your state residency and eligibility for reduced tuition. To qualify for reduced (that is, in-state) tuition and a *guaranteed* transfer to W&M, you must have lived in Virginia for at least a year prior to the beginning of the term you apply for. According to Virginia State law, proof of residency may include, but is not limited to, voting registration, actual voting, state taxes, permanent residence, employment, auto registration, or a driver's license.

As you have undoubtedly noticed from the discussion above, RBC, unlike most other back gateways, offers back gateway students on-campus housing. The school has its own "Student Village," with two residence halls, Freedom Hall and Patriot Hall, that reportedly offer all of the comforts of home and your choice of sharing accommodations in a two- to four-bedroom suite or living alone in a one-bedroom apartment. You may, of course, choose to be a commuter student by living off campus. For more detailed information concerning on-campus housing, visit www.rbc.edu/tuition.html.

For more information on the College of William & Mary, contact:

The College of William & Mary
Office of Undergraduate Admission
P.O. Box 8795
Williamsburg, VA 23187-8795
(757) 221-4223
Website: www.wm.edu
Email: admission@wm.edu

For more information on the Richard Bland College of the College of William & Mary, call Admissions at (804) 862-6249 or log on to www.rbc.edu/admissions.php.

# 24

## Finding Your Future at Georgia Institute of Technology

■ **KEYBOX**

**SCHOOL:** Georgia Institute of Technology

**LOCATION:** Atlanta, Georgia

**COLLEGE RANKING:** 36

**GATE POSITION:** Half-open

**SAT REQUIRED:** No

**HOUSING:** Yes

**MINIMUM AGE:** 18

**APPLICATION CRITERIA:** Moderate/High

**MEDIAN STARTING SALARY:** $58,900

**COST COMPARED TO FRONT GATEWAY:** Varies

I t was never very hard to find Tom when you needed him. All you had to do was look in the garage, where his dad had a workbench and a set of tools. Tom was always building things, especially ingenious little gadgets to make power tools do more. He even started selling some handmade accessories for a popular jigsaw model. The amazing thing was that Tom hadn't finished high school yet. Friends, neighbors, relatives, teachers, guidance counselors—everybody was telling him to start applying to colleges that had a good mechanical engineering program. It seemed a no-brainer.

But Tom wasn't so sure.

He wasn't sure he wanted to spend his whole college career slogging away in a math-heavy, no-frills, nose-to-the-grindstone engineering school. When a teacher suggested that he look into mechanical engineering at the Georgia Institute of Technology—everyone calls it Georgia Tech—Tom protested that it had a reputation as a "flunk out" school. Students were thrown into the deep end of the pool, intellectually speaking.

"Maybe," his teacher replied, "but Tech's program in industrial engineering is number one in the country and its mechanical engineering program is third."

"Well, maybe," Tom mumbled. "But my friend's older brother flunked out. 'Sink or swim,' they told him. And he sank. He transferred out as fast as he could."

Even the teacher had to admit that Tom had a point.

Georgia Tech is not for the faint of heart. As one of the nation's top engineering and technology schools—its College of Engineering was tied for fourth place with Caltech in the 2011 edition of *U.S. News & World Report*'s *Best Colleges*—Georgia Tech offers rigorous training in all aspects of engineering, in materials science, in computer science, and in architecture, and the school takes pride in its reputation for refusing to coddle anybody. Mere survival is considered an achievement in itself.

Tom's teacher wouldn't surrender to Tom's doubts.

"It *is* tough," he admitted. "It takes most students five, even six years to graduate, but then they leave Tech prepared for high-paying jobs in the kind of work you're *really* good at. Look, let me tell you about something." And that's when Tom learned all about the Dual-Degree Engineering Program and the Regents' Engineering Transfer Program (RETP).

## A "SELF-SELECTING" SCHOOL

The Georgia School of Technology was chartered on October 13, 1885, and welcomed its first class—all eighty-four students—in October 1888. Back then, it was not so much a college, let alone a university, as it was a technical vocational school. Founded in Atlanta, the post–Civil War South's most forward-looking city, Georgia School of Technology was intended to accelerate the entrance of the traditional agrarian South into the industrial economy that the rest of the nation was already profiting from. The school filled a need, and it grew rapidly, both in size and in scope. By the early twentieth century, Tech was no longer a trade school but had become a regionally recognized technological university. By mid century, its regional reputation had gone national, and in 1948 the school changed its name to Georgia Institute of Technology to reflect a new focus on cutting-edge technological and scientific research. Georgia Tech advanced in other ways as well, admitting women students in 1952 and, in 1961, becoming the first university in the Deep South to welcome African-American students without a court having ordered it to do so.

For years now, Georgia Tech has been the only technological university *U.S. News & World Report* consistently ranks among the top ten public universities in the United States. As mentioned, its College of Engineering was tied for fourth place nationally. Ranked first nationwide in industrial engineering, Tech boasted seven undergraduate engineering programs ranked in the top five for 2011 and nine graduate engineering programs ranked in the top ten.

Add to this lofty reputation the fact that, as a state university, Georgia Tech can be a real bargain (as of 2012, in-state students who maintained a B average got 90 percent of their tuition paid by the Hope Scholarship), and you would think an engineering degree was needed just to pry open the front gate. While it is true that *U.S. News & World Report* classifies Georgia Tech as "most selective," 51.2 percent of those who applied by January 2012 were accepted, a surprisingly high proportion for a school of Tech's reputation and value.

Not that the number tells the whole story.

"GT is a demanding school," the *Princeton Review* observes, "and the applicant pool is largely self-selecting." Consider that 81 percent of those admitted in 2009–2010 were in the top 10 percent of their high school class and achieved SAT composite scores in the 1230 to 1430 range. The conclusion is obvious: Overwhelmingly, it is the highest achievers who apply to Georgia Tech. Moreover, the graduation rate is low. Only 33 percent graduate in four years and 80 percent by six years. That dips to 79 percent at *eight* years. Not only is Tech demanding, but more than two out of every ten Tech students ultimately decide that the rigors of this school just aren't for them.

The great value of most back gateways is as a second chance for the majority of students who are turned away at the front gates of the nation's elite schools, but Georgia Tech is an elite university that actually accepts more applicants than it turns away. Make no mistake, nearly half of those high-achieving students who apply *are* turned away, and, for them, the back gateway is a very welcome alternative; however, the Dual Degree Engineering Program and the RETP are also great options for students like Tom—students who probably could get through the front gateway but who aren't sure they want to find themselves rudely plunged into the deep end of the pool the minute they step through.

## PREMIER RESEARCH UNIVERSITY

There's no doubt that Georgia Tech is one of the nation's premier technical universities. The 330-acre urban campus is a blend of old red-brick buildings on the east side and strikingly modern structures housing advanced classrooms and world-class research facilities in the central and west portions of campus. High-speed wireless access is universal across the campus, and all residence halls are extensively networked. Adjacent to the campus is Technology Square, opened in 2003, which offers pedestrian-friendly access to shopping, dining, and entertainment. Indeed, Georgia Tech's location in Midtown Atlanta gives students the run of a vibrant metropolitan area.

The Carnegie Foundation for the Advancement of Teaching classifies Tech as having "very high research activity." The school maintains close ties with large corporations and government agencies that provide extensive research funding, and the university's nonprofit research organization, Georgia Tech Research Institute (GTRI), sponsors advanced work in such specialties as radar, electro-optics, and materials engineering. Georgia Tech research has given birth to numerous start-up companies, and the school's Advanced Technology Development Center and VentureLab regularly assist faculty and graduate researchers and entrepreneurs in the work of corporate organization and commercialization. As of 2010, Georgia Tech was ranked by the Milken Institute fourth nationwide for spawning start-up companies, eighth in patents secured, and eleventh in technology transfer. Undergraduates are actively encouraged to participate in research alongside graduate students and faculty.

It is true that most Tech students accept or even proudly embrace being labeled as nerds, but the fact is that NCAA sports have also long been an important aspect of campus life. "Yellow Jacket" teams participate in seventeen varsity sports, including football, women's and men's basketball, baseball, softball, volleyball, golf, men's and women's tennis, men's and women's swimming and diving, men's and women's track and field, and men's and women's cross-country. Four Georgia Tech football teams were selected as national champions in news polls, in 1917, 1928, 1952, and 1990.

## TWO BACK GATEWAYS TO GEORGIA TECH

If you've been turned away from Georgia Tech's front gateway or if you just aren't sure you want to spend four (or more) years in the high-pressure environment of a hard-core engineering school, the College of Engineering offers two opportunities for beginning your college life outside of Tech.

The biggest and most popular back gateway program is the Dual-Degree Engineering Program. In this program, you enroll in and attend a participating liberal arts college for three years and then transfer to the College of Engineering at Georgia Tech for two. At the end of it all, you receive a B.A. from the first institution and a B.S. in engineering from Georgia Tech. At present, the participating schools are:

Agnes Scott College, Decatur, GA
Alabama A&M University, Normal, AL
Albany State University, Albany, GA
Armstrong Atlantic State University, Savannah, GA
Berry College, Mount Berry, GA
Clark Atlanta University, Atlanta, GA
Clayton State University, Morrow, GA
Columbus State University, Columbus, GA
Covenant College, Lookout Mountain, GA
Dillard University, New Orleans, LA
Elon College, Elon, NC
Emory University, Atlanta, GA
Fort Valley State University, Fort Valley, GA
Furman University, Greenville, SC
Georgia College & State University, Milledgeville, GA
Georgia Southern University, Statesboro, GA
Georgia Southwestern State University, Americus, GA
Gordon State College, Barnesville, GA

Jackson State University, Jackson, MS
Jacksonville University, Jacksonville, FL
LaGrange College, LaGrange, GA
Miami Dade College, Miami, FL
Montgomery College, Rockville, MD
Morehouse College, Atlanta, GA
North Carolina Central University, Durham, NC
North Georgia College & State University, Dahlonega, GA
Oglethorpe University, Atlanta, GA
Savannah State University, Savannah, GA
Spelman College, Atlanta, GA
State University of West Georgia, Carrollton, GA
Tougaloo College, Tougaloo, MS
Valdosta State University, Valdosta, GA
Wesleyan College, Macon, GA
Xavier University, Cincinnati, OH

You will find the experience at many of the participating institutions quite different from life at Georgia Tech. Berry College, for example, is a four-year liberal arts college located on an idyllic, 26,000-acre campus of gently rolling fields, lakes, and forests sixty-five miles northwest of Atlanta. While Georgia Tech enrolls more than twelve thousand full-time undergraduates, Berry has just 1,792 full-time undergraduates and a student to faculty ratio of 12:1. Instead of the large lecture classes you may expect in many Tech courses, Berry emphasizes small class sizes and a personalized learning experience. The acceptance rate is 63.9 percent. Dual-degree students at Berry can expect "the best of both worlds . . . the advantages and depth of a liberal arts education and a world-class technical education."

If you prefer another urban campus, Oglethorpe University, located in Atlanta, is less than ten miles from the Georgia Tech campus. A small institution, Oglethorpe has an acceptance rate of about 86.4 percent and enrolled more than one thousand full-time undergraduates in

2012, offering a student-to-faculty ratio of 13:1. Oglethorpe describes the dual-degree program this way:

> Engineering is a difficult subject. Students can maximize their chances for success by starting at Oglethorpe where the faculty's primary concern is effective teaching and working closely with students. With such a small faculty-to-student ratio, classes are small, and laboratories offer the opportunity for hands-on experience with sophisticated equipment. After three years of study at Oglethorpe, students transfer to the College of Engineering at Georgia Tech for two years to complete a Bachelor of Science in Engineering. On completion at Tech, students also receive a Bachelor of Arts degree from Oglethorpe.

The Dual-Degree Engineering Program is a 3/2 program—five years of schooling that result in two degrees. The College of Engineering also offers a four-year, single-degree, 2/2 program called the Regents' Engineering Transfer Program (RETP), a cooperative program between Georgia Tech and fourteen colleges in the University System of Georgia. These are:

Albany State University, Albany, GA
Armstrong Atlantic State University, Savannah, GA
Columbus State University, Columbus, GA
Dalton State College, Dalton, GA
Gainesville State College, Oakwood, GA
Georgia College & State University, Milledgeville, GA
Georgia Perimeter College, Clarkston, GA
Georgia Southern University, Statesboro, GA
Gordon College, Barnesville, GA
Macon State College, Macon, GA
Middle Georgia College, Cochran, GA
North Georgia College and State University, Dahlonega, GA

Savannah State University, Savannah, GA
Southern Polytechnic State University, Marietta, GA
State University of West Georgia, Carrollton, GA
Valdosta State University, Valdosta, GA

If you enroll in RETP, you will attend one of the participating institutions for your freshman and sophomore years, taking all of the mathematics and science courses as well as many of the engineering courses that are required in the first two years of the Georgia Tech engineering curriculum. When you have *successfully* completed the RETP requirements at the cooperating institution, you will be admitted to the College of Engineering at Georgia Tech to work toward completion of a bachelor of science in engineering degree. Advantages of enrolling in RETP include lower entrance requirements and the opportunity to attend a college that may be closer to home—a consideration if you are trying to reduce the total cost of your education. During your first two years at the cooperating institution, you will be invited to the Tech campus for campus tours, information sessions, and meetings with advisors in your engineering major.

## How to Apply

Neither the Dual-Degree Engineering Program nor the RETP automatically guarantees transfer to the College of Engineering at Georgia Tech. For transfer in the dual-degree program, you must successfully complete the three-year course work at the participating institution. For transfer in the RETP, you must complete a minimum of thirty semester hours (or forty-five quarter hours) that are transferable to Georgia Tech. Note that all of the courses required for transfer must be completed *before* you transfer; because they are actual prerequisites for admission to the College of Engineering, they cannot be taken at Georgia Tech. In both the dual-degree and RETP programs, faculty advisors will help to ensure that you select courses that satisfy the transfer requirements; however, you may want to preview the latest transfer requirements by consulting the checklist chart published online at www.admission.gatech.edu/images/pdf/Course RequirementsChart_2010101.pdf.

In order to be accepted for transfer, you will need to satisfy minimum GPA requirements at the cooperating institution. For most engineering majors, these minimums are 2.7 for Georgia residents, 3.0 for non–Georgia residents, and 3.5 for international students. Requirements for applicants in biomedical engineering, mechanical engineering, and computer science are higher: 3.0 for Georgia residents, 3.5 for nonresidents, and 3.8 for international students.

You will find detailed instructions for applying to the dual-degree program at http://coe.gatech.edu/content/dual-degree and www.catalog.gatech.edu/specialacademic/dual.php. Details about applying for RETP transfer are at www.catalog.gatech.edu/specialacademic/retp.php.

## TUITION AND HOUSING

Because the back gateway to Georgia Tech can be accessed through such a variety of participating dual-degree and RETP schools, tuition rates and housing options vary over the course of your education, depending on the cooperating institution you choose and on whether you elect the five-year dual-degree program or the four-year RETP. As with all cooperative programs, your tuition and on-campus housing costs are those charged by the institution you are currently attending. On-campus housing is available at Georgia Tech to both dual-degree and RETP students. As of 2012–2013, Georgia Tech tuition and fees were $10,098 in-state and $29,402 out-of-state; in-state students who maintain a B average are entitled to receive the Hope Scholarship, which pays 90 percent of tuition costs. Room and board was $11,440 for in-state as well as out-of-state students.

For more Dual-Degree Engineering Program information, contact:

Office of Undergraduate Admission
Georgia Institute of Technology
Atlanta, Georgia 30332-0320
(404) 894-4154
Website: www.gatech.edu
Email: admission@gatech.edu

Felicia Benton-Johnson, Ed.D.
Dual-Degree Engineering Director
(404) 542-3445
Email: felicia.johnson@coe.gatech.edu

For more RETP information, log on to www.catalog.gatech.edu
/specialacademic/retp.php and www.admission.gatech.edu/transfer/
#RETP.

# 25

# "City of Learning":
# University of California, Berkeley

---

### ▣ KEYBOX

SCHOOL: University of California, Berkeley

LOCATION: Berkeley, California

COLLEGE RANKING: 21

GATE POSITION: Half-open

SAT REQUIRED: No (but may be required for cross-registration programs)

HOUSING: Generally available (except for cross-registration programs)

MINIMUM AGE: 18

APPLICATION CRITERIA: Moderate

MEDIAN STARTING SALARY: $57,100

COST COMPARED TO FRONT GATEWAY: Varies

---

Despite critical economic woes in recent years, California's state universities remain one of the country's most admired systems of higher education, and the flagship of the California system has long been the University of California, Berkeley (UC Berkeley). Founded after the Civil War as a "City of Learning" near the state's most vibrant city, San Francisco, UC Berkeley radiates an aura of glamour rare among state universities and, since the early 1960s, has been associated with the forward-looking, freethinking, trendsetting, and sometimes radical culture of California's Bay Area.

While not everyone is comfortable with UC Berkeley's progressive outlook—and the university's students and faculty have never been reluctant to make some folks uncomfortable—you would be hard-pressed to find anyone who objects to the school's spectacular Northern California setting and its lush twelve-hundred-acre campus. The combination of intellectual freedom, cultural openness, and beautiful location has always attracted not only the best and brightest of students—statewide, nationally, and internationally—but a superb faculty that currently includes 227 American Academy of Arts and Sciences Fellows, 2 Fields Medal winners, 83 Fulbright Scholars, 139 Guggenheim Fellows, 87 members of the National Academy of Engineering, 132 members of the National Academy of Sciences, 3 Pulitzer Prize winners, 84 Sloan Fellows, 7 Wolf Prize winners, and 1 Pritzker Prize winner. Over the years, no fewer than 66 Nobel laureates have been affiliated with UC Berkeley as faculty, alumni, or researchers, and, at present, the active university faculty includes eight Nobel Prize winners. Indeed, the university honors its Nobel recipients with something highly coveted on every thriving college campus: perpetually reserved parking spaces, each marked with a special NL ("Nobel Laureate") symbol.

Landing a place among UC Berkeley's undergraduate student body may not be as hard as earning an "NL" parking spot, but it is by no means easy. One of the original "Public Ivies," UC Berkeley received a staggering 62,000 applications for the 2012–2013 freshman class and accepted some 13,000 of them—a little over 21 percent. If you find yourself one of the eight in ten who are turned away from Berkeley's front gateway, you will want to know about the two back gateway alternatives.

## ECONOMIC GROWTH AND SOCIAL INNOVATION

The "City of Learning" that opened its doors in 1869 had actually struggled into being three years earlier as the privately financed College of California. Finding itself cash-strapped even before it held its first classes, the school merged in 1868 with the state-run Agricultural, Mining, and Mechanical Arts College and, as the *University* of California, held its first classes in September 1869.

By the middle of the twentieth century, the American Council on Education ranked UC Berkeley second only to Harvard University "in the number of distinguished departments," but it was World War II that finally and dramatically catapulted the university to prominence in "big science" when one of its physics professors, J. Robert Oppenheimer, was appointed chief scientist of the Manhattan Project, creator of the atomic bomb. Since then, Berkeley has been in the forefront of U.S.-sponsored nuclear research and thermonuclear weapons development.

In recent years, the university administration has sometimes found itself in conflict with the liberal orientation of faculty and students because of the institution's growing reliance on financial support from big business and major industry. With state funding at a current low of about 25 percent, such giants as BP (a half-billion-dollar donor for biofuels research) and Dow Chemical ($10 million to research sustainability) are among the university's most important benefactors. Still, UC Berkeley proudly proclaims its ongoing commitment to foster economic growth *and* social innovation. Scientists on this campus discovered vitamin E and identified the first flu virus. And here also is where the nation's first no-fault divorce law was crafted. Despite controversy, UC Berkeley is today identified with breakthrough sociological research and the development of sustainable technologies in energy production and other fields. Rated by *U.S. News & World Report* twenty-first overall nationally in 2011, the university continues to hold its first-place *U.S. News* national ranking among *public* universities.

Berkeley does take that concept of a *public* university seriously. Like all other institutions in the California system, Berkeley is legally committed to accepting applicants based purely on merit, regardless of their financial means. For more than a century, financial aid has been available to students classified as "needy and deserving," and UC Berkeley has enrolled more federal Pell Grant recipients from low-income families than all eight Ivy League universities combined. In 2010, the school reported that a quarter of incoming freshmen were the first in their families to go to college.

UC Berkeley enrolled 36,142 students—25,885 undergraduates, 10,257 graduate students—as of fall 2011, who were being taught by 1,582 full-time and 500 part-time faculty in more than 130 academic departments and 80 "interdisciplinary research units." The institution's fourteen colleges are:

- College of Letters and Science: the largest college; encompasses more than sixty departments in the biological sciences, arts and humanities, physical sciences, and social sciences
- Haas School of Business
- College of Chemistry
- Graduate School of Education
- College of Engineering: includes departments of bioengineering; civil and environmental engineering; electrical engineering and computer sciences; industrial engineering and operations research; materials science and engineering; mechanical engineering; and nuclear engineering (chemical engineering is in the college of chemistry)
- College of Environmental Design: includes departments of architecture; landscape architecture; and city and regional planning
- School of Information
- Graduate School of Journalism
- School of Law

- College of Natural Resources: includes departments of agricultural and resource economics; environmental science, policy, and management; nutritional science; and plant and microbial biology
- School of Optometry
- School of Public Health
- Richard and Rhoda Goldman School of Public Policy
- School of Social Welfare

As of fall 2009, the most popular majors were electrical engineering and computer science; political science; molecular and cell biology; environmental science, policy, and management; and economics.

## BERKELEY'S BACK GATEWAYS

Incoming Berkeley freshmen are overachievers. About 98 percent of those accepted in fall 2011 were in the top tenth of their high school class, with the median high-school GPA for admitted freshmen standing at 4.19 on a 4.0 scale because of the profusion of AP classes they take. For the many truly superb students who don't get through the front gateway, there are two entrances—maybe two and a half—in the back.

### Back Gateway #1: The College of Engineering Junior Transfer Admission Program

Subject to availability of space, the Junior Transfer Admission Program admits students who have satisfactorily completed a minimum of sixty transferable semester units (or ninety quarter units) at a California two-year community college or any accredited four-year college or university to "advanced standing" in the College of Engineering. Once admitted, you will have just four semesters at Berkeley to complete your degree—

though, with approval from the dean, you may secure an additional semester, and special consideration may be granted to those who need additional time due to illness or learning disabilities. Entrance requirements are fairly stringent:

1. Because space is limited and applications always exceed Berkeley's capacity to accommodate them, California residents who attend a California community college "are currently given special consideration over applicants from four-year colleges."

2. You must choose a specific engineering major at the time of your application for transfer. You may not transfer as an "undeclared" student. This means that you need to understand the various engineering fields and the majors associated with them before you apply. You will *not* be permitted to change your major after you have been admitted.

3. The UC Berkeley engineering faculty will evaluate your application based mainly on the completeness of your "lower-division" (that is, freshman and sophomore) preparation and your level of academic achievement as expressed in your GPA. You must have completed the equivalent of all required core Berkeley preparation courses before you apply, and it is recommended that you also complete as many other lower division courses required for graduation as possible. Doing so will greatly strengthen your application. Engineering faculty members *in your declared major* carefully review your personal statement that is required as part of your application. They look "for evidence of interest in [your] chosen major and thoughtful match between the academic program and [your] academic and career objectives."

4. Other considerations for admission include the total credits you have earned. If you have earned more than eighty-nine credits at four-year colleges or universities, you may be considered too advanced for admission to the bachelor's program in engineering. Preference is also given to U.S. citizens, those who attend Cali-

fornia two-year community colleges, and those who have a record of "unusual achievement," leadership, community service,
relevant employment, and "special talent."

5. Neither test scores nor letters of recommendation are required or
requested.

6. The UC Berkeley Office of Undergraduate Admission and Relations with Schools maintains articulation agreements with California community colleges that specify equivalencies between
your school's courses and those required for transfer to the UC
Berkeley College of Engineering. It is important that you work
closely with your college counselors to ensure that you have met
course requirements and have established a strong record before
applying for transfer.

Admittedly, the back gateway restriction to the College of Engineering may seem severe, and it is certainly a deal breaker if you have
absolutely no interest in engineering. Bear in mind, however, that the
range of majors within the engineering college is broad and includes
offerings from the departments of bioengineering; civil and environmental engineering; electrical engineering and computer sciences; industrial engineering and operations research; materials science and
engineering; mechanical engineering; and nuclear engineering.

### How to Apply to Back Gateway #1

Admission to the UC Berkeley College of Engineering Junior Transfer
Program is competitive. Remember that admission decisions are greatly
influenced not just by *your* qualities as a student, but by the quality of
the entire applicant pool *and* the number of spaces that are available in
the program when you apply. This availability depends in part on your
intended major, so it *may* be a wise strategy to choose a less popular
major to increase your chances of admission. Be aware that the great
benefit of the back gateway is the valuable opportunity to develop your
academic chops at a less expensive and less competitive two- or four-

year school before transferring to the more costly and more intensely competitive environment of UC Berkeley.

To get detailed information on the Junior Transfer Program, consult:

- Your college advisors or your college transfer center
- The UC Berkeley Office of Undergraduate Admissions (www .admissions.berkeley.edu)
- Engineering Student Services at (510) 642-7594

When you are ready to apply for transfer, be sure to log on to www .admissions.berkeley.edu for applications, application procedures, and deadlines. In addition to supplying you with the latest information you need, the site includes links to an online application and other necessary forms.

## Back Gateway #2: General Transfer Students

As competitive as admission is, the College of Engineering at UC Berkeley *actively seeks* junior transfers. UC Berkeley also considers transfer applications to any of its colleges, not just engineering. The problem is that, while about 20 percent of the undergraduates throughout the state's university system are transfer students, UC Berkeley receives disproportionately more applications for transfer than any other school in the system. Every year, many more students apply than Berkeley can accommodate. So while transfer to the College of Engineering is quite competitive, transfer to other UC Berkeley colleges is an even longer shot. In fall 2012, for example, 15,745 students applied for transfer, and 3,819 were admitted. At 24 percent, this acceptance rate is marginally better than that for front gateway freshman admissions. Still, transfer does offer a second chance, gives you more time to prepare academically in a less competitive environment than UC Berkeley, and, depending on the school from which you transfer, may save you money. Moreover, as with the Junior Transfer Program offered by the

College of Engineering, preference is given to applicants who are California residents attending a California community college. These applicants are given special consideration over applicants from four-year colleges and universities, including applicants from other UC schools. Thus, if you are applying from a two-year California community college, your chances of being admitted as a transfer student are almost certainly better than the overall 24 percent. Of course, you still have to meet the academic requirements and make the cut. In arriving at their decisions, Admissions Committee members consider:

- Your GPA (In 2010, for instance, the GPAs of admitted transfer students ranged from 3.61 to 3.97.)
- Your having completed freshman and sophomore prerequisite courses for your intended major
- Your "grade trends" (falling or rising?)

Note that transfer admission requires you to have completed a minimum of sixty transferable semester credits; however, most programs will not consider applicants who have *more* than eighty credits—unless all course work was completed at a two-year college. In addition to these basics, your application will also be judged on:

- Demonstrated interest in the major for which you are applying
- Personal qualities such as leadership and motivation
- Extracurricular accomplishments
- Employment record
- Potential for making a contribution to the intellectual and cultural vitality of the campus

### How to Apply to Back Gateway #2

Get started by logging on to www.universityofcalifornia.edu /admissions/transfer/index.html. After reviewing the information you find there, you can apply online at www.universityofcalifornia.edu/

admissions/how-to-apply/index.html. Here you will be able to check your eligibility, ensure that you meet deadlines, review available majors, prepare your personal statement, fill out the online application, and pay the required application fee.

## ONE MORE IDEA: A "HALF" GATEWAY

There is one more entrance onto the Berkeley campus you should know about. As of fall 2010, UC Berkeley had "cross-registration" agreements with California State University East Bay (Hayward); Mills College, Oakland; San Francisco State University; Sonoma State University; Holy Names University; John F. Kennedy University; and Dominican University of California. In addition to these programs, which have been established for some time, a new program created by California State Senate Bill (SB) 1914 makes it possible for students from the campuses of the California State University or Community College systems to attend classes at Berkeley. By participating in cross-registration or taking advantage of the new program, you have an opportunity to "try out" UC Berkeley even as you demonstrate your ability to excel in that school's demanding course work. This is a very effective way of increasing your chances of being accepted as a transfer student before you graduate.

Eligibility requirements for cross-registration vary somewhat, depending on what school and department you are applying to and depending on your host school. In general, however, you will be required to submit a cross-registration permit to both the host school and to UC Berkeley. If you have at least a 2.0 GPA and are a full-time sophomore, junior, or even a senior, you are eligible to participate in the program. You will be asked to furnish transcripts, letters of recommendation, and test scores in support of your application.

To qualify for a cross-registration permit, you must register only for UC Berkeley courses that are not offered during the same semester at your home school, and you must meet all prerequisites and criteria for the cross-registered course. In addition, you will not be permitted to enroll in independent study, tutorial, or individual instruction courses while you participate in cross-registration with UC Berkeley. Requirements and restrictions for the program created by California State Senate Bill (SB) 1914 are less stringent, but your ability to take courses at UC Berkeley is subject to availability of space and approval of your home campus. The program is available to California residents only.

## TUITION AND HOUSING

The total cost of your four-year education depends on the tuition and other fees charged by the institution from which you transfer. In many cases, these costs will be lower than those at UC Berkeley, especially if you are transferring from a two-year California community college. For 2012–2013, yearly in-state tuition and fees at UC Berkeley were $13,392; out-of-state tuition was $36,078. A year's room and board was a steep $15,448 in-state and out-of-state.

On-campus housing at UC Berkeley is generally available for full-time transfer students, but not for cross-registered students or those attending classes under the SB 1914 program.

For more information, contact:

Office of the Registrar
University of California, Berkeley
120 Sproul Hall, #5404
Berkeley, California 94720-5404

Mills College
5000 MacArthur Boulevard
Oakland, CA 94613

(800) 87-MILLS
Email: admission@mills.edu

California State University, East Bay (Hayward)
(510) 885-2784
Email: admissions@csueastbay.edu

San Francisco State University
1600 Holloway Avenue
San Francisco, CA 94132
(415) 338-6486
(415) 338-3880
Email: ugadmit@sfsu.edu

Sonoma State University
Division of Student Affairs and Enrollment Management
1801 E. Cotati Avenue
Rohnert Park, CA 94928
Website: www.sonoma.edu/admissions/

Holy Names University
3500 Mountain Boulevard
Oakland, CA 94619
(510) 436-1000
Website: www.hnu.edu

John F. Kennedy University
(800) 696-5358
Website: www.jfku.edu

Dominican University of California
(415) 457-4440
Website: www.dominican.edu

# 26

## Dream Bigger:
## University of Notre Dame

> ### ■ KEYBOX
>
> SCHOOL: University of Notre Dame
>
> LOCATION: South Bend, Indiana
>
> COLLEGE RANKING: 17
>
> GATE POSITION: Ajar
>
> SAT REQUIRED: Yes
>
> HOUSING: Not guaranteed
>
> MINIMUM AGE: 18
>
> APPLICATION CRITERIA: Moderate
>
> MEDIAN STARTING SALARY: $55,300
>
> COST COMPARED TO FRONT GATEWAY: Varies

Not every movie is a fantasy. In 1993, director David Anspaugh released *Rudy*, a film about Daniel Eugene "Rudy" Ruettiger, a young man who grew up in working-class Joliet, Illinois, dreaming of playing college football at the University of Notre Dame, a school legendary for the sport. Rudy was a decent high school player, but at five feet, six inches and 165 pounds, he was hardly in line for a football scholarship, and he had neither the money nor the grades (he was later diagnosed with dyslexia) to get into Notre Dame any other way.

Or so he was told—over and over again.

The movie depicts Rudy setting aside his dream and instead going to work in a steel plant. The real-life Ruettiger served two years in the navy after high school, then worked in a power plant. At last deciding to revive his Notre Dame ambitions, he applied, was rejected, and instead enrolled at Holy Cross College, located, like Notre Dame, in South Bend, Indiana. After two years at Holy Cross, he applied for transfer to Notre Dame and suffered three rejections before finally being admitted in 1974.

As a transfer student, Rudy Ruettiger had found a back gateway into the school of his dreams. To this day, Notre Dame encourages transfers from any accredited school, including Holy Cross, but the university has formal dual-degree programs with only a handful of schools. They may offer just the back gateway you are looking for.

## LOFTY ACADEMIC REPUTATION

Ranked seventeenth among national universities by *U.S. News & World Report* in *Best Colleges 2013*, Notre Dame has long been listed among the nation's top twenty-five institutions of higher learning by *Princeton Review, Time, Kiplinger's,* and *Newsweek*. In addition to its lofty academic reputation, the school is one of the few universities that is consistently ranked among the top twenty-five in the U.S. Sports Academy Directors' Cup standings, which rate the best overall athletic programs. In 2007, *Princeton Review* put Notre Dame among the top five "dream schools" in a survey of parents of college-bound students.

Little wonder that the school accepted just 24.3 percent of those who applied by the end of 2011. You should also know that, year to year, 21 to 24 percent of those who are admitted are children of alumni. Thus, more than two out of three high-achieving high school seniors with visions of joining the Fighting Irish instead endure the painful disappointment of rejection.

Father Edward Sorin, a native of France, was just twenty-eight when, on November 26, 1842, he and seven other members of the newly established Congregation of Holy Cross accepted from the Bishop of Vincennes (Indiana) 524 acres in St. Joseph County, Indiana, at the south bend of the St. Joseph River. As he later explained, Father Sorin "dreamed of building a great university in honor of Our Lady." On January 15, 1844, he secured from the Indiana state legislature a charter for L'Université de Notre Dame du Lac (The University of Our Lady of the Lake).

By the early twentieth century, Notre Dame was renowned as a center of aerodynamics research, the development of radio technology, and the formulation of synthetic rubber. In the 1920s, a new president, Father James A. Burns, already noted as an educational theorist, dramatically revised the curriculum and teaching methods. He also established the university's law school as one of the leading legal programs in the nation.

Today, Notre Dame encompasses five colleges. All undergraduates enroll in one of these after attending, as freshmen, the First Year of Studies program, a common curriculum designed to provide a foundation from which they can launch into their declared major. After completing the First Year, a student may enter:

- The College of Arts and Letters, which includes twenty departments in the fine arts, humanities, and social sciences; students may earn a bachelor of arts in any of thirty-three majors
- The College of Science, with five departments (biology, chemistry, mathematics, physics, and pre-professional studies) that award a bachelor of science degree
- The School of Architecture, a five-year undergraduate program that awards a bachelor of architecture degree
- The Mendoza College of Business, offering course work in accountancy, finance, management, and marketing
- The College of Engineering, with five departments: aerospace and mechanical engineering, chemical and biomolecular engineering,

civil engineering and geological sciences, computer science and engineering, and electrical engineering; the college awards B.S. degrees to undergraduates and also serves, through its dual-degree program, as the back gateway into Notre Dame.

## THE RELIGIOUS CHARACTER OF THE UNIVERSITY

Although religious affiliation is not a criterion for admission to the University of Notre Dame, some 80 percent of undergraduates do identify themselves as Catholic, and the Catholic character of the campus is evident in its numerous Catholic clubs, ministries, and church-affiliated volunteer organizations. Each residence hall has a resident priest and contains a chapel, where Sunday Mass is celebrated. Nevertheless, participation in religious activities or services is not compulsory, and the university encourages students of all religions and denominations to form their own organizations.

All Notre Dame presidents have been and will almost certainly continue to be priests from the Holy Cross order, but, since 1967, when governance of the university was put into the hands of a lay board rather than the Holy Cross congregation, it has been board members who select the president from a pool of Holy Cross candidates. While Notre Dame is today a major research university, with a strong scientific program, it is also a center of the Congregation of Holy Cross and maintains on campus Moreau Seminary, the order's principal seminary.

## THE BACK GATEWAY TO NOTRE DAME

As with a number of the nation's other elite schools, the back gateway into the University of Notre Dame is a dual-degree program involving the College of Engineering and partner institutions. Unlike other such arrangements, however, Notre Dame offers a 3/2 as well as a 4/1 option.

In a 3/2 program, you study for three years at the partner school, then complete your engineering studies at Notre Dame in your fourth and fifth years. At the end of your fifth year, you are awarded two degrees: a bachelor of arts or bachelor of science degree from the partner institution (some partner institutions offer only a B.A.) and a bachelor of science in engineering degree from Notre Dame. Currently, the 3/2 partner institutions are:

Assumption College, Worcester, MA
Bethel College, Mishawaka, IN
Carroll College, Helena, MT
Elon University, Elon, NC
Goshen College, Goshen, IN
Loyola University, Chicago, IL
Saint Anselm College, Manchester, NH
Stonehill College, Easton, MA
University of Saint Thomas, Houston, TX
University of Saint Thomas, St. Paul, MN
Xavier University of Louisiana, New Orleans, LA

The 4/1 dual-degree program is available through a special partnership agreement with just one school, Saint Mary's College, in South Bend (actually, in the unincorporated community of Notre Dame northeast of South Bend proper). If you choose this program, you, as a Saint Mary's student, will take a combined curriculum of Saint Mary's science courses and Notre Dame engineering courses beginning in your sophomore year. After four years, you will graduate from Saint Mary's College with a B.A. or B.S. degree, then go on to Notre Dame to earn a bachelor of science in engineering degree in your fifth year. An important restriction of this program is that Saint Mary's is a women's college, and, therefore, the 4/1 program is available only to women.

Engineering at Notre Dame offers a broad array of degrees and concentrations:

- The Department of Aerospace and Mechanical Engineering offers B.S. degrees in aerospace engineering and in mechanical engineering, with undergraduate concentrations available in aerospace engineering (for mechanical engineers); bioengineering; computational engineering; control and mechanical systems; design and manufacturing; energy; materials; solid mechanics; and thermal and fluid sciences.

- The Department of Chemical and Biomolecular Engineering awards a B.S. in chemical engineering, a certificate program in materials, and three curricular sequence options (in biomolecular engineering, environmental chemical engineering, and premed).

- Students in the Department of Civil Engineering and Geological Sciences can work toward a B.S. in civil engineering or in environmental geosciences. They must also select a concentration in either structural or environmental engineering as part of their course of study.

- The Computer Science and Engineering Department offers degrees in computer engineering and computer science. Students in the department may specialize in one of three concentrations: bioinformatics and computational biology, information technology leadership, and media computing.

- The Department of Electrical Engineering awards a B.S. in electrical engineering and offers undergraduate concentrations in communications, energy, multimedia, and semiconductors and nanotechnology.

Stonehill College is typical of the 3/2 partners participating in the dual-degree program. A small Catholic college (2,600 full-time undergraduates in 2012) located on a lovely 375-acre campus on the outskirts of Boston, Stonehill offers more than seventy academic programs and a dedicated faculty of top-notch professors. The school describes its curriculum as "rigorous," and *U.S. News & World Report* classes it among the "more selective" of the nation's institutions. In 2012, the college accepted 65.2 percent of those who applied. Not only are the entry requirements more liberal than those for Notre Dame, tuition is also significantly lower. For 2012–2013, a year at Stonehill cost $35,110 in tuition and $13,310 for room and board, compared to $42,971 and $11,934 at Notre Dame.

The five-year dual-degree program allows students to complete three years at Stonehill College and two years at Notre Dame to earn a B.A. (not a B.S.) from Stonehill and a B.S. from the University of Notre Dame in any of the engineering fields offered by the College of Engineering. Like many other partner schools, Stonehill does not promote itself as a back gateway into Notre Dame, but as an opportunity to prepare for a career in engineering while amassing a strong academic background in liberal arts. This, Stonehill explains, not only creates an individual with a genuinely liberal education, it produces a job candidate that many businesses today find most attractive—a professional who approaches a technological field from a background of humane learning.

When you enter Stonehill as a freshman, you will begin taking courses in the Cornerstone Program, a core curriculum designed to enhance "critical thinking, effective communication, social responsibility, and personal growth and discovery." Also in your first year, you will be required to select a science major and start taking science and math classes in your chosen major. During years two and three, you will complete the Cornerstone Program with courses in a foreign language, natural and social sciences, ethics, and a three-part Learning Community, while you continue to take math and the science courses. Transfer to Notre Dame takes place after your third year at Stonehill, and your two degrees are awarded after completion of your fifth year.

Saint Mary's College, the only partner institution that participates in a 4/1 dual-degree—four years at Saint's Mary's (with some course work at neighboring Notre Dame) and a fifth year at Notre Dame—has long been known as the "little sister" of the University of Notre Dame. This all-women school was founded in 1844 by the Sisters of the Holy

Cross and has a student population of 1,555 full-time undergraduates. The partnership with Notre Dame is called a dual-degree program, but it might also be characterized as a co-exchange program, since you take a significant amount of course work at Notre Dame even while you are enrolled at Saint Mary's.

Like Stonehill, Saint Mary's is considered a "more selective" institution and was ranked at number eighty-seven among national liberal arts colleges by *U.S. News & World Report* (2013); however, 84 percent of those who applied in 2011–2012 were accepted. Costs are even lower than at Stonehill. For the 2012–2013 academic year, tuition was $33,280, with room and board adding $10,140.

As mentioned, the important restriction on this program is that you have to be female to enroll in Saint Mary's. As a dual-degree student, you will take at Saint Mary's all of your pre-engineering courses (such as chemistry, mathematics, and physics) in addition to the liberal arts courses necessary to satisfy Saint Mary's four-year degree requirements. All actual engineering courses are taken at Notre Dame, and you may begin these as early as your sophomore year. Indeed, as you work toward your two degrees, you will almost certainly find yourself taking an increasing number of your classes at Notre Dame, even before you formally transfer.

Saint Mary's strongly encourages students majoring in the sciences and mathematics to apply for the dual-degree program, but it is open to students in any major who fulfill the necessary prerequisite course work. The Saint Mary's website advises that the curriculum is "strenuous and demands the best efforts and careful planning of well-prepared, highly motivated students," but the website also points out that the "program offers the best of both worlds since students enjoy small classes, personal attention from faculty, the supportive environment of a women's college, and a strong liberal arts education at Saint Mary's" as well as the "excellent technical training and access to cutting-edge facilities" at Notre Dame.

Ideally, you should make your decision to enter the dual-degree program by the end of your freshman year at Saint Mary's, but after the first two years of pre-engineering courses, you are *required* to officially declare your intent to pursue an engineering major at Notre Dame. Although there are no guarantees of admission, "the dual-degree program is structured to support your application," and Notre Dame "has agreed to grant admission to the Saint Mary's College students who, after three and a half years of study, have earned at least a 2.5 GPA (on a 4-point scale) in their technical courses and who have been recommended by Saint Mary's." You will be notified of Notre Dame's decision by March 1 of your senior year.

## How to Apply

The procedures for applying to the 3/2 dual-degree program vary somewhat, depending on the partner school; however, acceptance of transfer by the Notre Dame College of Engineering requires:

- A cumulative GPA of at least 3.3
- A grade of at least C in all courses
- A minimum of sixty credit hours that can be transferred to satisfy Notre Dame's engineering requirements
- Recommendation for admission by the chair of your major department at the partner institution

The requirements are less stringent for Saint Mary's students in the 4/1 dual-degree program and call for a minimum GPA of 2.5 in technical courses. If you apply from Saint Mary's, you will be required to submit a preliminary plan for course work and to work closely with academic advisors from both Saint Mary's and Notre Dame. The actual process of transfer is, however, streamlined for Saint Mary's applicants. Notre Dame requires only the official college transcripts and the transfer application form, waives the requirement for high school transcripts, and does not require standard examination scores or personal statements (the "essay").

## TUITION AND HOUSING

Your tuition and other costs will be those charged by the partner school for the first three years of the 3/2 program or by Saint Mary's College for the first four years of the 4/1 program. Once you transfer, the University of Notre Dame will levy charges according to its schedule and policies, but it will also provide you with the same level of financial aid and scholarship opportunities offered to other transfer students.

For 3/2 dual-degree transfer students, on-campus housing is based on availability and is not guaranteed. Nevertheless, you may always access an inventory of off-campus accommodations through the school's Office of Student Housing. Because Saint Mary's College is a neighbor to the Notre Dame campus, Saint Mary's guarantees on-campus housing to dual-degree students for all five years, in an effort to foster the "strong friendships and networks to support them throughout."


For more information, contact:

University of Notre Dame
Notre Dame, IN 46556
(574) 631-5000
Website: http://nd.edu/admissions/

Assumption College
500 Salisbury Street
Worcester, MA 01609
Kathleen Murphy

Dean of Enrollment
(508) 767-7285
Website: www.assumption.edu

Bethel College
1001 Bethel Circle
Mishawaka, IN 46545
(800) 422-4101 (menu option 2) or (574) 807-7600
Website: www.bethelcollege.edu

Carroll College
601 North Benton Avenue
Helena, MT 59625
(800) 992-3648 or (406) 447-4533
Website: www.carroll.edu

Elon University
Elon, NC 27244
(800) 334-8448 or (336) 278-3566
Email: admissions@elon.edu
Website: www.elon.edu

Goshen College
1700 South Main Street
Goshen, IN 46526
(800) 348-7422 or (574) 535-7535
Email: admission@goshen.edu
Website: www.goshen.edu

Loyola University
1032 West Sheridan Road
Chicago, IL 60660
(800) 262-2373 or (312) 915-6500

Email: admission@luc.edu
Website: www.luc.edu

Saint Anselm College
Office of Admission
Saint Anselm College
100 Saint Anselm Drive
Manchester, NH 03102
(888) 4-ANSELM or (603) 641-7500
Email: admission@anselm.edu
Website: www.anselm.edu

Stonehill College
320 Washington Street
Easton, MA 02357
(508) 565-1000
Website: www.stonehill.edu
Email: admissions@stonehill.edu

Saint Mary's College
Notre Dame, IN 46556
(574) 284-4000
Website: www.saintmarys.edu

University of Saint Thomas
3800 Montrose
Houston, TX 77006-4626
(800) 856-8565 or (713) 525-3500
Email: admissions@stthom.edu
Website: www.stthom.edu

University of Saint Thomas
2115 Summit Avenue

Mail 32F
St. Paul, MN 55105
(651) 962-6150
Email: admissions@stthomas.edu
Website: www.stthomas.edu

Xavier University of Louisiana
Office of Admissions
Xavier University of Louisiana
1 Drexel Drive
New Orleans, LA 70125
(877) XAVIERU or (504) 520-7388
Email: apply@xula.edu
Website: www.xula.edu

# Index

# About the Author

C. W. Henderson has been an international education researcher specializing in college admissions for more than a decade, including doctoral research in both the United States and the UK. Currently he is a Ph.D. candidate and voting member of the American Educational Research Association. He is executive editor of the educational research publications *Ivy League Week*, *Education Business Weekly*, and "Education Letter" in the *Wall Street Journal* professional edition. As a researcher and writer focusing on Ivy League and elite college admissions, he has edited more than one hundred articles on this topic. In a cover story, *USA Today* named him one of "6 Who Made a Difference." At his *Open the Gates* blog at www.openthegates.com he has updates on college admissions including back gateways to top colleges. Email cw@openthegates.com to contact the author.